Hunting Camp
Memories

North American Hunting Club
Minnetonka, Minnesota

HUNTING CAMP MEMORIES

Copyright © 1998 North American Hunting Club

Mike Vail
Vice President, Products and Business Development

Tom Carpenter
Director of Book and New Media Development

Dan Kennedy
Book Production Manager

Heather Koshiol
Book Development Coordinator

David R. Maas
Editor

Larry Anderson
Illustrations

Ian McMurchy
Cover Onlay Photo

Zins Design Studio
Book Design and Production
    Scott Zins
    Ingrid Lang

ISBN 1-58159-024-5
10 9 8 7 6 5 4 3 2 1

CONTENTS

Introduction 4

I Swear It's True 7

Deer Hunting Adventures 89

Hunting with Family & Friends . . 121

First Hunts to Remember 221

Introduction

Bill Miller, Executive Director—
North American Hunting Club.

The Waldo Gang Camp was established at the head of a beaver pond on KC Creek in northern Wisconsin's Marinette County in 1911. A teenage Alfred John and his uncle ventured north on the railroad with all their gear and enough provisions for a 10-day hunt packed into a large wooden crate. That crate also contained a couple of narrow-gauge train wheels. When the pair arrived in the small town of Goodman, they bought a 4x4 timber at the lumber mill and fastened it to the bottom of the crate. They attached the wheels to the ends of the timber and towed their camp into the woods on one of the many logging spurs off the main railroad line.

Thus began a hunting camp tradition that lasted until 1987. That's the last year NAHC Member Bob Holbrook and I towed his camper trailer the 8 miles off the pavement to park it under the giant pine which had shaded the Waldo Gang Camp each November.

For those hunters who passed through the Waldo Gang Camp in those 77 seasons, that hallowed ground spawned countless memories of the events and camaraderie of deer hunting. I recollect those memories like most folks recall nursery rhymes ... wonderful, exciting and touching stories told annually by the seasoned elders at camp. (And that was almost everyone, since the next youngest hunter toward the end was my dad, and he didn't have me until he was 42!)

We hope that every NAHC member is fortunate enough to have such a fount of hunting camp memories. If the contributions we received for this book are any indication, then that hope is fulfilled. This book is a celebration of those memories past and of the sincere wish that you create more in each coming season.

Take care, good hunting ... and good memory-making.

Bill Miller

Bill Miller
Executive Director
North American Hunting Club

I SWEAR IT'S TRUE

It seems like every hunting
story holds a twist—some-
thing special, unique or odd—
that adds an element of surprise
and intrigue.

Without these elements of
chance, hunting (and hunting
stories) wouldn't be quite so
interesting. In fact, some hunting
stories focus on the twist itself:
something so different, so out of
the ordinary, that it *becomes*
the story.

That's what the following
memories are about—those
hunting camp yarns that the
teller prefaces with, "I swear
it's true, but once …"

Gun Rack

by Mark Molling
Waukesha, Wisconsin

A few years ago, during the Wisconsin gun deer season, Harry, a coworker of mine, was sitting along a ridge looking over several deer trails when he noticed another hunter walking toward him. The hunter approached and asked, "Have you seen a buck run past carrying a gun?"

Not believing what he had just heard, Harry asked the hunter to repeat what he had said.

"Have you seen a deer run past here carrying a gun?" he asked again.

"No, I haven't. When did the deer start carrying guns around here anyway?"

The hunter explained that he had been hunting an area about a mile away. He saw a nice looking eight-point buck coming down a trail and had taken what he thought was a good shot. The deer dropped in its tracks right on the trail. He approached the deer and touched it lightly with the barrel of his gun. The deer did not move, and the hunter placed his gun across the deer's antlers. As he was getting his camera out of his pack to take a picture, the deer suddenly stood up, shook its head, noticed the hunter standing there, and ran off with the gun in its antlers. For several minutes, the hunter just stood there, stunned by what had happened. He then began his search for the armed buck.

A few days later, Harry saw the hunter again. He was still looking for the deer and his gun.

The Imaginary Bear

by Bart Varca
Mamaroneck, New York

This is a story that happened about 25 years ago while deer hunting in the mountains of lower New York State. We had our regular group of guys: George, Bob, Sal, Cal and myself. Cal was a local resident who lived on a farm about a mile away. George brought along a friend, a newcomer named Charlie. He was a friendly type of guy who lived in a big city all his life, and he was a complete novice to any form of hunting with no experience being in the woods. Charlie was excited to come along and try it out, and he convinced George to bring him up to camp for deer hunting.

On the night before opening day, we were all sitting in camp talking about our past hunting experiences. You could see Charlie was getting into these stories, especially Cal's. Cal was born and raised in these mountains and had taken all types of game the mountain offered. Charlie asked Cal, "How did you get that bear I saw mounted in your living room?" With that question, Cal told of how he was deer hunting on the upper ridges of the big mountain directly behind our camp. Being a very mild afternoon, he had sat down against a tree and dozed off. He was quickly awakened by the roar and growl of a big black bear standing tall on his rear legs only a couple of feet from him. At this point in the story, Cal let out a roar and a growl to emphasize to Charlie how the bear sounded. We could practically see the hair on the back of Charlie's neck stand on end. We all knew Cal had shot that bear with a long shot on a different mountain in a different county ten miles away, but he was pouring it on and priming Charlie, telling him to be very aware and alert when in the woods and to watch out for all the roaming bears when out deer hunting.

Cal's story must have stayed on Charlie's mind into the next day. While we were out hunting, he seemed very nervous. He wouldn't sit still by himself for very long, and whenever we posted him on a stand, he would move to make sure he was close to one of the other fellows. This went on all morning. That afternoon, George, Cal, Charlie and I made our way to the upper ridge of the mountain, with Sal and Bob posting directly below us in the lower woods. It was our plan to sit along this ridge and for Cal to go to the top, walking through the buck brush to spook out the hiding deer. We expected the deer to run down and along the ridge when coming off the top. Before Cal moved out he told Charlie, "You know, Charlie, this is the ridge where I shot that bear and that's the tree I slept under," pointing to a large oak nearby.

Charlie's face went stark white and he didn't want any part of this post. I took it instead. George was going north on the ridge for about 200 yards, and I told Charlie to go south from me for a good distance and sit down, knowing he would be back close to me within the hour.

George got the first crack at a buck after about 30 minutes, and when two does came running by me I knew George had taken the buck out of the group. I gave Charlie (who really wasn't that far away) a quick wave to come over as I intended to help George field dress the buck. It was a nice six-pointer, and George had all the work done when we arrived. He placed the deer liver and heart into a plastic bag, tied it closed and handed the bag to Charlie telling him, "This is our supper for tonight. You carry it along with our guns, and Bart and I will drag the deer. It's getting late and we should hurry since we have about three miles to go."

By the time Cal came down to the edge of our ridge, he could see George and me several hundred yards downhill dragging the deer. Charlie was lingering behind, struggling with our guns and holding the plastic bag with an extended arm. All of a sudden, Cal let out two chilling bear roars that echoed downhill through the woods. George and I knew it was Cal, but not Charlie. All day long Charlie had anticipated that a bear was watching him and waiting to spring on him at any time.

He thought for sure this was the bear coming to get him, especially since he was carrying the bag of bear vittles. His only thought was to get his legs moving and get the heck off this mountain. He dropped the bag, dropped the guns and ran past us like an Olympic sprinter yelling, "Bear coming! Bear coming!"

We tried shouting at him, telling him to stop, but his mind was set and he was hell-bent on getting back to camp. Cal came down to join us, laughing up such a storm that he could hardly walk straight, espe-

©ANDERSON···

cially when we told him what was in the plastic bag. We picked up the bag and the guns and continued downhill to join up with Sal and Bob. They said Charlie had come through their area still running at top speed and still yelling, "Bear coming! Bear coming!"

It was dark when we arrived at camp. It was also dark inside the cabin and the door was locked. When we called for Charlie, he answered from inside but wouldn't open the door. I used my key and found Charlie sitting in the dark, all sweated up, trying to catch his breath and pouring himself a stiff drink. When we asked him why he took off like he did, he said that he had heard the bear and *seen* it too.

"Are you sure you weren't imagining seeing the bear?" we asked.

"No way," said Charlie. "It wasn't my imagination. I saw a black bear right behind me and he was coming after me and that plastic bag."

We weren't able to convince Charlie that it was Cal's antics in combination with his imagination—that there never had really been a bear. For the rest of the week Charlie became our camp cook, clean up and house boy, and no matter what he was doing he did it within sight of the cabin. At the end of the week we gave Charlie an award for not only being a good sport, but for being the fastest downhill runner these mountains had ever seen.

It is now several years later and the fellows are all gone except for Cal and I. We have relived the incident many times and still wonder if it really was Charlie's imagination. Cal loves to tell the story when we have a group of hunters together. In his mountain drawl and hearty laugh, he tells about running Charlie and that plastic bag. When he finishes telling how serious Charlie was, he points his finger to me and says, "Now, ain't that right, Bart?" Of course I smile and nod my head in agreement, but deep in my mind I still wonder, was there a bear behind Charlie? I guess we will never know.

Hunting Adventures with Freckles

by Charles Stevens
Center Point, Texas

I'm 63 years of age and look forward to hunting season each year. I have hunted most of the legal game, but have grown to favor quail hunting over a good bird dog. I had a good brace of pointers to begin with but had to sell them when I traveled overseas with my unit of the Air Force. I have since hunted with setters, German shorthairs and Brittanys.

A skeet-shooting friend of mine gave me a Brittany pup, which I named Freckles. I trained him on a lease located a few miles east of Eden, Texas, where my friend and I hunted quail. Both bobwhite and blue quail populated the ranch, and wild turkeys also frequented a local roost and fed on the ranch.

At the beginning of Freckles' training, he thought that he could catch a quail on the wing. He ran the pads right off his feet chasing. Once he found that he couldn't catch a bird in flight, he began to chase cottontail rabbits. Once I convinced him that rabbit chasing was for beagles, not bird dogs, he settled in to pointing quail for me.

There was one particular hunt that I will never forget. I had been seeing turkeys at the water trough, approximately two or three hundred yards inside the gate at the lease. I never wanted to involve Freckles in turkey hunting, but I wanted one of the fine, long-beard gobblers. On this particular day, I took my deer rifle along and thought that if I saw them, I'd take a long shot and see if I could bag one.

As I drove through the gate I noticed a nice flock of turkeys at the water trough. I dismounted from the truck, placing it in park, and left the motor running. I sneaked out into the bushes and attempted to get the crosshairs lined up with a long neck or head. If you have ever done this you know that it is just about impossible. I kept trying to get closer when I spooked them and they ran. I followed them for some distance and finally just shot into the air to scatter them, so that I could maybe call one to me later. About that time, I heard a vehicle coming down the dirt road. I thought that it was probably one of the ranch hands coming to feed the sheep that were pastured there. Lo and behold, it was my truck!

Freckles must have gotten excited when he heard my shot and started jumping around and put the thing in gear. I ran to the truck and attempted to open the door on the driver's side and found Freckles had locked it. The truck was headed for a large prickly pear bed and some trees. I ran to the other side and grabbed the door. It was locked as well. I closed my eyes as the truck hit the patch of pricklies and some small trees and the engine died. Using my hunting knife, while standing in the middle of a prickly pear patch, I was able to get the wing vent open and unlock the door. There was little damage—just a small dent and a slow leak in one tire. I felt bad that I had made such a foolish mistake, and I apologized to Freckles for never teaching him to drive.

Outfoxed

by Charles Clark
Ransomville, New York

Some years back my father purchased a walker hound to use for fox hunting. My older brother and I did likewise, and we went fox hunting on the weekends almost every week. The dogs were not the best, but they were fairly good and we ran quite a few fox.

One Sunday, with several inches of snow on the ground and the sun shining brightly, we went to try our luck. Not long after we entered a large woodlot, the dogs struck a fresh track and got a fox going. They took it across an orchard, an open field, another orchard and into the next woodlot. Knowing the fox would circle, I quickly crossed the field and sat down with my back up against a large woodpile on the edge of the second orchard. My theory was that when they brought the fox back, he would break out of the orchard, cross the field and head back for the woodlot where he had started.

I could hear the dogs in the distance, and suddenly their voices became louder and I could hear them heading my way. I sat still with shotgun ready, intent on getting Mr. Fox when he hit the open field. Suddenly, the dogs were in the orchard behind me, heading right my way, but the fox did not show. When the dogs reached the woodpile, they started milling around, seemed confused, and after several minutes took off on a track heading back into the orchard, but not in the direction from which they had come, I knew then that the fox had outsmarted me.

17

Upon further investigation, I found the
fox tracks headed directly toward the woodpile. But
instead of going around it, he had climbed up on it, probably to get a look around. The tracks crossed the top of the
woodpile and showed that he had sat down on the woodpile directly
over and behind the spot where I was sitting. While I was waiting for
him, he was just sitting there, probably laughing at me. When the dogs
got close, he jumped off—behind me of course—and ran off. I've often
thought of what a picture this would have been with a hunter sitting,
waiting for the fox to show, while the fox sat on a woodpile behind him,
looking down at him.

A Doe to Remember

by Arthur Bennett
Watkins Glen, New York

On the fourth day of gun season, I was out hunting in the woods. I had gotten out of my truck, walked to where I wanted to be, and was just standing there catching my breath when I looked up and saw a large rack of antlers. I took a shot and hit the deer in the back. The deer went down. I walked up to the deer, preparing to field dress it. When I lifted the back leg, I suddenly realized it had no male fixtures. This deer was a doe.

I left the woods with the deer, stopped home to show my wife (who was amazed), and then went to have the deer weighed for the deer pools I had entered. The deer weighed in at 177 pounds and had eleven points. Every place I stopped to show my doe/buck, people were skeptical. They weren't sure what to call it. Of course, I received more than my share of teasing and bad jokes.

I had pictures taken of it and called in the Department of Environmental Conservation. They checked it out twice and were also amazed. Everyone from hunters to law enforcement personnel wanted to see this doe deer with antlers.

After showing it off and explaining for the next two days, the newspapers ran several stories about my unusual deer. I am having the head and "back end" mounted.

New Gloves

by James Woods Jr.
Boise, Idaho

For many years now, my brother, friends and I have been on a number of hunting trips in Idaho. Some were uneventful, producing nothing more than the camaraderie shared by good friends and good stories around the fire. Some, on the other hand, were very eventful.

One of my funniest deer hunting trips happened way back in 1979 and included my brother, Ed, and my uncle Joe. We were hunting up around Idaho City for mule deer. On opening morning, my brother and I took separate forks in a trail that would eventually meet at the top of the mountain. Joe was hunting farther down the mountain.

A shot rang out and I turned to see that Ed had just bagged a nice three-point mulie. When we reached the deer, Ed didn't want to get his new leather gloves wet, as there was about seven inches of snow on the ground. So he put one glove on each antler and proceeded to turn the deer over, when the buck suddenly decided it wasn't dead and sprang to its feet, running down the hill toward where Joe sat. Minutes later, when we reached the spot where the deer had crossed close to Joe, we asked him why he hadn't shot at the deer.

He said, "What deer?"

I said, "The one that just ran by."

He said, "Oh, that deer! Well, there was no way I was shooting a deer that is smart enough to wear gloves on his antlers to keep warm, because he may be smart enough to have a gun and shoot back!"

The thought of watching that deer go by had us laughing all the way back to camp.

We managed to find the deer the next day. Unfortunately, my brother had to buy a new pair of gloves as the deer must have decided he was warm enough and tossed the gloves away.

The One that Got Away

by Luis Hilligoss Jr.
Danville, Illinois

In 1976, my father, my brother and I scheduled our first Iowa pheasant, rabbit and quail hunting trip. It was fun and exciting. Since that time, my brother and I have carried on this hunting tradition and made many more trips to Iowa. But the last three years we have hunted in Kansas. The following story happened on one of those Kansas hunts.

My brother, a few hunting buddies and I arrived the day before the season opened to obtain our non-resident licenses, check out the land and find a place where we might get permission to hunt. On Saturday morning, we decided to hunt a milo field next to some railroad tracks. We arrived just before sunrise. It was a cloudy, cold and windy morning, and we placed one man on the edge of the right-of-way, one man in the right-of-way and the other three men in the milo about 15 rows apart. I was carrying one of my favorite firearms, a Browning over/under 12 gauge. We had hunted about 15 minutes when a freight train came from the opposite direction. We waited for the train to pass by. When there were about eight boxcars left, we resumed our hunt. All of a sudden a cock pheasant exploded into the air about 15 yards in front of me and headed straight up. Instinctively, I took aim and pulled the trigger. The pheasant folded up and landed on top of a box car! We were all surprised and joked about "the one that got away."

22

The 200-Meter Downhill

by Mark Hardy
Gastonia, North Carolina

This particular April morning began like most others when visiting my parents' home ... quite early! "So, are you going to sleep all day?" is the typical question one hears at 5:30 a.m. at their house. I've never really understood my dad's incessant need to be awake before most North American farmers. "Thanks, Dad. After checking the fire, maybe you should go and shake that delinquent rooster awake!" was my unusually witty reply that morning.

Even though I grumbled around the kitchen for about a half an hour, Dad knew that it was mostly for effect. After all, it was opening morning of spring gobbler season. We had been talking about and planning this morning for months, as much as two hunters can plan anything concerning turkeys, that is. We knew of a hollow about an hour's drive from home that had been a roosting area for years. Dad assured me that these turkeys, their grandfathers and their grandfathers' grandfathers had roosted in this hollow. This morning was going to prove all turkey hunting articles wrong. We joked about the game warden throwing us in jail for shooting these "poor defenseless creatures." All of this talk during breakfast and the drive over did not begin to prepare us for the day's events.

After sitting in the "perfect hollow" for four hours, it was quite plain that no turkey or any of his ancestors, relatives, friends or even mild acquaintances were roosting or feeding anywhere near where I was sitting. Dad and I were going to meet at 11:00 a.m. Around 10:30, I heard him, or what I thought was him, coming up the ridge toward me. The sound was coming directly toward me. Just before I caught a glimpse of Dad coming from my left, four turkeys ran to the right. They had been the sound.

We quickly formulated a master scheme that would surely lead to the demise of one of these foolish birds. We would both drop off the sides of the ridge, below the crest, and try to jump them up between us. With two masterminds in the woods, that poor old jake didn't stand a chance. Just as planned, he got up between us, and the sound of two shotguns going off filled the mountain air. The bird fell from the sky like a wet bag of flour. He thumped on the ground between us. We trotted up the ridge, both sure of our own expert marksmanship.

We were laughing and retelling our versions of the final seconds of this successful hunt when we noticed that the turkey's head was slowly wagging toward a more stationary position atop its neck. We were still unconcerned but decided that a Buck knife sliding across the bird's neck may not do a lot for the turkey, but it would help stabilize our nerves. As Dad unsnapped the sheath of his knife, the bird started down the ridge like Jesse Owens coming out of the blocks. Now I'm no Olympic sprinter, but I felt sure that I could chase down a wounded turkey. I'm not sure if it was a false start or not, but whatever the reason, I was slow leaving the starting line. Dad immediately did the sensible thing and threw up his gun, but it was too late. So it was off to the races.

For a bird with major head trauma, it ran a very respectable 200 meter race. We crashed off that ridge at breakneck speed. The poor turkey was bouncing off trees and bushes, and I was steadily gaining ground. Knowing when to make your move in a race can make all the difference. Finally, the ridge ended in a very steep-sided hollow. The bird fell off a small ledge the final four or five feet of the ridge. Little did he know that right behind him, a 155-pound juggernaut had just gone airborne. My size 8.5 Adidas hiking boot landed at the base of his neck. I never knew that you could pull a groin muscle crossing the finish line in a turkey race.

Dad and I still argue about who actually killed that turkey. He insists that his model 12 shooting number 4s got him, and I still say that my 8.5 Adidas took him out.

My Wife Terry's Only Deer

by Don Johnson
Myers Chuck, Alaska

Here in southeastern Alaska, we call deer up with blat calls, especially in the rut. Just about everyone has one of these calls, so the deer do get used to them. But I had purchased a grunt tube and was anxious to try it out, because nobody else in our community had one yet.

Having a skiff as our only means of getting around, the tides mean a lot. I had an hour before high tide, so I ran up into the woods about 100 yards or so. I hadn't gotten the second grunt out of the tube before a nice buck came charging through the brush. He stopped and started sneaking back when I took a heart shot.

I found a little blood but quickly lost the buck's trail. I went back home, got Terry, my wife, and our big malamute, and headed back out. I figured Terry could keep our skiff from going dry, and give me directions from the woods. Perhaps the dog would earn his meals.

I told Terry that if she heard me yell, to yell back and I would know which way to come out. We have iron mountains all around, and a compass is worthless.

After giving up on the dog, who was just chasing squirrels around, I started searching again. After about 15 minutes, I heard yelling and commotion from down at the beach. I was too far away to understand any of it, but I could tell something exciting was going on.

I charged as fast as I could back to the beach, and when I looked about 60 yards out into the water, there was a deer towing my 16-foot Boston Whaler at about three knots. I couldn't believe my eyes. Our dog

26

was swimming beside the boat, barking and biting at it. This action really seemed to excite the deer.

What happened was this. The deer ran into the water after being discovered by the dog. Then Terry took the skiff out, caught up with the injured deer, dangled the bow line in loops around its antlers, and then tied back the rope to the cleat. She gave up on killing the deer with a couple of hard blows with the ax. She said it just made him mad. Somehow she managed to get the dog into the boat.

I yelled at her to stand in the stern and hold the dog. I took a rest over a stump, and stopped the forward progress of the skiff with one carefully placed shot. The buck was ours.

The Other Side of the Story

by John Caknipe
Chase City, Virginia

I t was cold and raining, so I decided to drive my old pickup the ¾ mile to my favorite treestand. I had a spot where I could park it out of sight, so off I went.

By noon I was in my stand. When I got there, I had a plastic grocery bag to cover my seat so I wouldn't have to sit directly on the wet stand platform. I positioned myself and pulled up my rifle. I was ready. I was so excited that every crack in the woods and brown leaf became a deer. I needed to relax. I was also getting wet and cold.

The first hour passed without seeing any movement. Then the second and third hours. The temperature began to drop and occasionally I could see sleet mixed with the rain. By 4:00, the rain had stopped. It was definitely getting colder. Around 5:00 it began to rain again. This time it was a heavy rain with a lot of sleet.

With only 45 minutes left of shooting light, I decided to stick it out. After all, I'd already been there five hours. Why not?

Suddenly my senses went into overdrive. I was startled, but I didn't know by what. I looked and saw nothing. My instincts told me to look back. As I slowly turned to look over my shoulder, there, not 25 yards away, stood three big bucks. One was a ten-point, the second was a six, and the third was a huge spike. They were playing in the rain, jumping up and down and chasing each other around like little puppies.

I slowly eased my rifle to my shoulder. At contact, I laid my cheek on the stock and eased off the safety. Placing my finger on the trigger guard, I took my eyes off the deer and looked into the scope. What a shock. All I could see was me. My entire scope and the top of the rifle had collected about a half-inch of ice.

I had a flush mounted scope, but I figured since they were so close I could just aim down the side of the barrel. The ice seemed pretty uniform all the way down it. But no matter how I tried, I could not position myself at such an awkward angle to get a clean shot. I had to move. I had to turn around.

I clicked the safety back on and reached out with my hand to steady the movement as I started to move ever so slowly. Then came the noise. I was frozen to the platform and the plastic bag sounded like someone was rattling tin as I twisted to get free. Ice began to fall off the platform and shatter on the ground below.

Needless to say, the deer took off. Interestingly, they ran right under my stand and straight away from me. I raised my rifle, but now that I had turned, it was just as awkward shooting back behind me again. I fired. It looked like my bullet hit about five or six feet to the left of the big buck. No time for a second shot.

After a moment of catching my breath, I decided to call it a day. All the racket surely had frightened anything close enough to be seen by dark. I turned back around in the stand, unloaded my rifle and lowered it to the ground. I eased over the side, placing my foot firmly on the ladder. Slowly, I eased down to the next step, but not easy enough. Both feet shot off the board and I was dangling in the air. But for only a second, I had no grip with my hands either. Crash! I hit the ground.

Carefully picking up my bruised body, which had slid about ten feet from the stand, I moved to get my rifle. As I bent over to pick it up, down the slope I went again. The next time I kneeled. Slowly, I worked my way back to the truck. Between the cold and the ice, every bone and muscle in my body ached.

The old truck started on the first try. I turned the heat on high and waited for the windshield to thaw. Finally, I was ready to go home to a hot cup of coffee and a warm house. As I began to back up to turn around, my truck developed a mind of its own. I applied the brakes, but that only seemed to cause it to pick up speed. I was on a solid sheet of ice. I was going downhill—backwards. I was heading for the highway.

I turned the wheel, applied all the brakes (even the hand brake), but nothing slowed my progress. The truck hit the highway and slid across and came to rest in the ditch on the other side. Then slowly, the front end joined the rear in the ditch.

That was the "icing" on my day. I locked the doors and walked the 250 yards home. Inside, I made a pot of coffee and turned on ESPN to watch a hunting show.

Alaska, 40 Years Later

by Stan Kokolus
Coplay, Pennsylvania

My first big game hunt was for Dall sheep in Alaska in 1957. Since that trip, I've hunted Alberta, the Yukon, Nova Scotia, Newfoundland and Wyoming. But one of my most memorable hunts took place recently in Alaska. I was hunting in October of 1997 with my friend—outfitter Butch King—and his guide Dale. On the ninth and final day of my brown bear hunt, we awakened to find clearing skies and a light coat of snow on the ground. We left camp and got to our lookout just before daybreak. It was about a 30 minute walk. We had been glassing for about 15 minutes when Dale said, "There is our bear in the river and heading downstream. The wind is perfect. Let's go!"

We hurried down to the river, which took about 30 minutes, and then started moving downstream. We finally got to the pool where we last saw our bear, and he was gone. Dale found his tracks and we continued on, checking out each river bend with caution. Suddenly, Dale sighted the bear about 150 yards from us. We dropped our packs and started crawling until we were about 90 yards from the bear. I crawled past Dale to the edge of a grassy area. I fired one shot from my .375 H&H with a 300 gr. Nosler partitioned bullet. I hit the bear in the front shoulder, and took out his heart and lungs. He made one attempt to get up the bank, but he fell back into the water and splashed a little. Then it was all over.

Dale thought it was a good bear for the last day of my hunt. Later, I asked Dale how far he was going to track this bear. He replied with a grin, "As long and as far as it would take."

31

We had not had a look at the bear to judge yet, but he had a nice, big footprint. We realized we had a big bear when we started pulling him out of the water and onto the shore. Dale had a tough pack ahead after skinning, but he is a tough man. Butch picked us up that evening, and it was a treat to be back at the lodge. Butch scored the bear's skull at $29^{12}/_{16}$. The hide squared to 10 feet, 6 inches.

How Much Wood Could A Woodchuck Chuck?

by Gary Lewis
Bend, Oregon

By the time we had bought bows, arrows, hunting tags and supplies for the trip, there wasn't much money left for camo gear. Figuring that if it was good enough for the army ten years ago it was good enough for us, we bought surplus army clothes with other men's names sewn into them. With a couple sticks of old face paint thrown in, we were ready for our first season bowhunting.

As it happened, we were the only archers in the campground adjacent to the high mountain meadows where we were hunting. We soon found out that wearing face paint and old camouflage is not the best way to inspire confidence in your fellow campers.

A seven-year-old named Joseph was the first to break the ice. He rode up on his bike and I saluted him. "Hello, Joseph." I, being the expert woodsman I am, spotted the name on his license plate. Henceforth, Joseph was convinced that I was no ordinary bowhunter. I'm not sure if it was because he knew I was literate or if he thought that I could know his name by looking at him (the latter was the impression that I tried to make).

"What are you Army guys doing up here, anyway?" Joseph asked. We explained that these were just old Army fatigues and that we were bowhunting. He seemed skeptical.

"Huh! I ain't never heard of Army fat-I-gews."

According to Joseph, he was an extremely accomplished hunter for his tender age. He spoke of a rabbit that he had harvested, innumerable barn swallows and the odd groundchuck. I didn't ask why he wanted to pick on odd groundchucks. As he spoke, it became evident that he was no ordinary seven-year-old. Finding in us a fascinated audience, each adventure he related was more fantastic than the last.

He recalled the time that his mother had hung a carrot in the front of his archery target (for no apparent reason). It seems that as he let the arrow fly, a rabbit leapt into the air for the carrot. The hapless hare was impaled upon the shaft, which still retained enough velocity to carry forward into the bull's-eye! An astounding feat of arms by anyone's book.

Authentication of this and other stories proved somewhat difficult, however. When his mother happened on the scene, no doubt to protect her innocent child from bowhunters, Joseph developed a strong desire to go fishing.

"But you don't like to fish," she said.

"I do now."

I did, though, manage to find out the answer to one age-old question before he walked away.

"Joseph," I said. "You seem to be a great outdoorsman." He nodded solemnly. "You must know a lot about animals." Again the modest affirmative. "There is something I have wanted to know since I was your age."

Like all great students of the wild, he was eager to be of help, to answer any question a novice might have.

"Joseph," I said slowly and carefully, "How much wood..." He nodded as if to encourage me, his pupil, "...would a woodchuck chuck if a woodchuck could chuck wood?"

He thought it over. It was, after all, a question that required deep thought and must be answered with tact. He didn't want to hurt my feelings just because I was naive.

"Nine," he said with all the authority he could muster. "Two if it is a little one."

The Tag that Almost Got Away

by Mary Kay Rausch
Addy, Washington

Several years ago, my husband, Pete, was lucky enough to take my 80-year-old father, Ray, on his last elk hunting trip. This was also Pete's first such trip.

The going joke around camp that year was that Pete was sure to get his elk, because every time Dad brought someone new to the camp at Colockum Pass, near Ellensburg, Washington, that person always got an elk, much to everyone else's disgust.

Well, Pete lived up to their expectations and got a really nice six-point bull on his third day out. He laughingly told Dad and my brothers that it was because he had stayed in camp a little later than the rest of them, to eat just one more of my great chocolate chip cookies!

Well, the real part of the story takes place the following day when they heard some yelling going on near their camp. My oldest brother, Gary, and his friend Steve were still in camp as their tags weren't good until the following day. They came running and yelling for Dad to get ready to head out, that someone below their camp had seen a small herd of bulls headed their way. Dad came out of his nice, cozy, warm tent and, not feeling much like hiking out much further, grabbed a camp chair and his rifle and sat down. With a big smile, he said, "Well, you never know, I might just get lucky. I've seen them run through camps before!"

Sure enough, three big bulls, each one a five-point, came charging

35

out of the woods into an open clearing right out in front of their camp. Pete grabbed my dad and showed him where they were running across the clearing. Dad threw up his rifle and said, "Where?" Pete showed him again, and he got off a shot. Nothing! He took aim and threw another shot at the lead bull, dropping him right there!

Well, you can imagine the excitement in that camp!

Gary and Steve took off to get out to the elk before someone else decided to claim it, yelling at Pete to hurry and get Dad's tag. Dad, in his haste, gave Pete what he thought was his tag—only he really handed Pete his game card!

When Pete ran out to the elk, Gary was heading back to camp to get Dad and walk him out to the elk so everything was legal, should a game agent happen by. He yelled over his shoulder, "Someone should cut that elk's throat and tag it!" That someone was either Steve or Pete.

Neither of them had a gun or a hunting knife with them, as Pete was done hunting and Steve couldn't start until the next day. As Pete leaned over and started to tie the tag on, he noticed two things. First, that it was the game card and not the tag, and second, that bull wasn't as dead as they had thought!

Pete and Steve looked at each other, then Steve handed Pete his pocket knife with a silly grin on his face. Pete looked at that big bull laying there with his head turned under his shoulder, and then looked down at that little ol' pocket knife, and told Steve that before he reached down there to cut that elk's throat he wanted to make sure he wasn't too lively. Pete reached out and grabbed one of the elk's tines. He wiggled that horn just a little—that was all it took—and that bull started to lift his head, shaking it, and started struggling to get up. Pete and Steve jumped back and stood there watching with their mouths hanging wide open, amazed, as that darn bull stumbled up to his feet, swaying a little like he was dizzy. He started walking away.

Pete said that his first thought was to jump him and bulldog him down because he was still so stunned from the rifle shot that hit him right across the top of his spine. Thank goodness he decided that the bull was just too big to wrestle with. After the first few steps, the bull moved into a trot, disappearing off into the woods as Pete and Steve stood by helplessly.

As Pete and Steve walked toward camp, Gary saw them and yelled for them to stay with the elk. Coming into camp, Gary and Dad wanted to know, "What are you doing leaving that elk out there alone?"

Pete just looked at them and said, "Well, he got up and walked off!"

"What do you mean he walked off?" they both asked.

I think everyone was as disappointed as Dad that day, disappointed that Dad didn't get to take home that one last elk, disappointed in themselves that they just got too excited with Dad's shot, and they all went out there virtually empty-handed.

The going joke in elk camp now is, "Make sure they're dead before you hang that tag on!" because if they would have had Dad's tag instead of his game card, that elk would have walked off with a tag flipping in the wind!

Opening Day

by Dean Fay
Rochester, Washington

It was early October and three weeks before deer season. The weather was ideal for scouting, so I skipped school. My nephew and I counted forty-some deer that day, marked the locations of the good ones on a DNR map and planned for opening day.

That evening at dinner, my dad asked how school had gone that day. I should have known better because he was never one to ask a question without reason. I lied. I said that school was fine. Maybe it wasn't a lie. Just because I hadn't been there didn't mean that it wasn't fine. In fact, it may have been a better place for my being gone. When Dad said that he had talked to my principal, I knew that I had dug a hole and jumped in. I confessed my sin in the hopes of getting a little less punishment. I told Dad how many deer we had seen and showed him our map. All he said was, "Good. I wouldn't want you to waste your time."

The next morning, I was back in school and telling everyone who would listen that I had cut classes and my dad had gone along with the scheme. Of course, I had to do my time after school for a couple of days, but I had the feeling that I had won the battle without much effort. Over the next couple of weeks, Dad and I did the normal scouting and even used the same map that I had placed my marks on during my day away from school. We picked out a camp spot and accumulated a pile of firewood for opening weekend. Things were looking good. Dad never mentioned the skip and I felt that I was home free. I have to admit that at about this time I was thinking that I might be able to get by with similar jaunts away from academia in the future.

The night before season was a ritual at our home. Dad would come home from work and we would pack the truck with food and camping gear for the morning trip to camp. It was a time when old family hunting stories dominated the talk. To a high school kid, it was pure excitement. If I had paid closer attention, I would have noticed that my ammunition had not been included and my hunting clothes had been returned to the closet.

The next morning, I was in a big hurry. My alarm had not gone off, even though I knew I had set it. As I scrambled out the back door, Dad started the pickup and warmed the engine. It was dark, but the dome light was on and I could see him plainly. As I ran up to the passenger door, he reached across the cab and pushed the lock button down, put the Ford in reverse and backed out of the driveway. I was too stunned to chase the truck, and I stood in the dark watching the taillights disappear down the road.

I walked back into the kitchen and poured a glass of milk. On the table was a note. It said, "I wouldn't want you to waste your time hunting deer today. Mr. Rocky needs a ditch dug. He will be by at eight. Be ready." Mr. Rocky was my principal. He didn't hunt. But then, neither did I that day.

Mr. Rocky's "ditch" seemed more like a canal. The ground was rocky, and I picked as much as I shoveled, but I finished about six that evening. I crawled into the front of his truck and thanked him as he handed me somewhat less than minimum wage for the work. He seemed to enjoy my predicament. I didn't care. By the time we were on the highway, I was sleeping.

I woke when he shut the motor off and I stumbled out into the darkness, dropping my money off my lap. It wasn't much, but I had more than earned it, so I got down on the ground and tried to find the change in the dark. Several minutes passed before I realized that there were others around the truck. Mr. Rocky was talking to my dad and a couple of the neighbors. When I heard the principal say that he didn't know what he would do with the ditch, I came wide awake. I had been had!

Today, as I look back over the day—lost hunting, ditch digging and conniving adults—I have to admit that it was a lesson well learned. I didn't see it quite that way at the time, but maturity allows me to laugh at myself now. Mr. Rocky drove home after a cup of coffee and unloading my gear from the back of his truck. I went to bed listening to the snickers of the other hunters.

The next morning Dad and I shot matching four-pointers within thirty minutes of each other. That somehow made things better. It was some time before I lived down the ditch-digging, though. That Christmas there was a gold painted shovel under the tree instead of the usual box of shells. Christmas night, however, when I went up to my room, there was a wonderful Remington 870 shotgun leaning against my bed.

Mohammed Ali of Turkeys

by Bob Carberry
Auburn, New York

My friend John met me at the local Dunkin' Donuts for coffee to plan our strategy. I already knew what my plan was because I had been awake most of the night thinking about it. We arrived at our hunting area well before daylight and headed to our predetermined locations to get set up. It was still dark and I was leaning against a large tree, finishing my coffee and again praying that this hunt might work out the way I had planned. I figured the law of averages was on my side. My decoy was placed on the edge of a green field and a picked corn lot, about 25 yards from my location. The tree I was leaning on was at the top of a steep incline, which led down to the river below. As the sun began to come up, I could hear the sound of the water running below me. I wondered if I'd be able to hear a turkey gobble with all the racket. About 30 seconds went by and my question was answered. Coming from behind me and on the other side of the water, a tom sounded off so loud my hair stood up. I quickly remembered what had happened earlier that month when Mr. Tom wouldn't cross the water. I figured I had nothing to lose, so I grabbed my box call and let go with five soft yelps. Not only did that bird sound off again, but two other birds started gobbling. The first bird was somewhere behind me and the other two were already coming toward me from another direction. I couldn't believe what was happening. All month long I wasn't able to get one bird to come to me, now I had three birds coming at once, and all from opposite directions. I was trying to figure out what way to face and was quickly running out of time. Then I remembered what my hunting partner told me once. He said the dominant tom usually gobbles first. I turned around just in time to see Mr. Tom

My tom did a somersault and ended up
heading back out across the field.

step out into the picked corn, his beard dragging on the ground and me stuck in an awkward position. He was about 35 yards from me when he noticed my decoy. He went into full display, and I decided it was now or never. I don't know exactly what happened next. I was starting to slide down the embankment and attempting to get my gun into position when old tom must have figured something wasn't quite right. He shrunk back down from being in full display and made a beeline back toward the safety of his woodlot. He had just about three steps to go when I got myself stabilized, lined up my sights and let one go. What happened next, I wish I had captured on a video. My tom did a somersault and ended up heading back out across the field. He was attempting to get airborne and was able to get up about three feet off the ground. I guess I didn't want to ruin my trophy, so I didn't shoot again. He seemed to be moving in slow motion, and I just knew I could run him down. I left my gun on the ground and took off on a dead run. I was on an intercept course. I had a good angle on him and our paths met about 40 yards out, me running for all I was worth and him flying with everything he had left. I made a leaping tackle and we both landed on the ground. Tom was flapping and kicking and I was trying to grab anything I could. At that point, I wasn't sure who was going to win the fight. During all the commotion, I grabbed his beard, but that came off in my hand. When I did get him by his feet, he was kicking, flapping and pecking me so hard I wasn't able to hold on to him. It flashed through my mind, "Just my luck. I had to pick the Mohammed Ali of turkeys."

When our battle finally ended, I don't think anyone would have been able to tell who won just by looking at us. My turkey and I were both on the ground, and I wouldn't have taken any bets on who looked better. As I regained my strength, I collected my hard-earned trophy and started to make my way back up the hill toward my truck. It was about 6:15 a.m., and I couldn't believe my eyes when I looked and saw an old woman in a bathrobe standing at the top of the hill by the road. She was looking in my direction, and as I approached her, the only thing she said was, "That's the funniest thing I've ever seen."

At that, she turned, crossed the road, and headed back toward her house. I sat down with tom and waited for John to join us. When he did, he took some pictures for me and we both laughed uncontrollably as I told him what had taken place.

My first trophy tom now resides in a place of honor at my home. He's not alone there, but his story surely sits alone at the top of my hunting camp memories.

Beeware

by Edwin Sampsell III
Montgomery, Pennsylvania

It was one of those beautiful mid-September days when it feels good to just get out of the house and enjoy nature. Also, with archery season in Pennsylvania fast approaching, I was well overdue for some serious scouting. I told my wife I was going to the mountains to blow some stink off and do a little scouting.

After dinner I put on a long-sleeved flannel shirt and my hunting boots, and headed for the mountains. I parked my truck along Route 15 (a major highway) and started hiking up into the mountains to look for deer sign. After approximately an hour of hiking, I found a spot with some buck rubs and lots of deer droppings. This was the spot where I was going to spend the evening hours watching for deer.

I was not prepared for what happened next—in more ways than one. After the nice dinner and an hour of hiking, my body was telling me that it was time for a nature call. Since this was a spur-of-the-moment trip, I did not have any toilet paper with me, or any other of the items I normally carry while hunting. Since I was so unprepared, I started looking around for some of nature's own toilet paper. I found a nice patch of soft green ferns around an old dead log. I dropped my drawers and proceeded with the business at hand while combing the mountainside with my eyes for deer. Suddenly, I felt something moving around down below, and as I looked down I was shocked and scared. There were ground hornet-type bees crawling all over my bare bottom. I took one hand and covered where I did not want to get stung the most and made a hasty retreat while shedding all articles of clothing.

There I was in all my glory, standing stark naked in the mountain with nothing on but my boots. I had been stung approximately 15 times. I was afraid of getting sick from the stings and I couldn't go to the truck naked; I was parked along that major highway.

I went back and retrieved my clothes with a stick. I put each article of clothing on a flat rock and stepped on every inch and then shook off the dead bees. I made it back to the truck and drove home. When I reached the house, I was not walking too well. It looked like I was a cowboy who just got done riding a six-foot wide horse. I entered the house walking funny. My wife, who is an RN, asked me what was wrong. I told her I needed help in the bedroom. After some wise cracks, she finally came back to the bedroom where I stood already naked. After a few more wise cracks, I told her I had a serious problem and it wasn't about sex. When she finally saw the bee stings and heard the story, she attended to my numerous stings while making smart comments the whole time. I had no reaction to all the stings and I was very glad it was cool out that day, as the bees were moving rather slowly.

What I learned from this encounter I pass on to all outdoorspeople: Do not make a nature call in the woods until there have been a few hard frosts!

Lost Lighter

From the Norway, Maine Advertisor-Democrat
Submitted by Skip Durant
N. Waterford, Maine

The first week in November, John Meister's brother was visiting, trying his hand at a bit of deer hunting. He got lucky and bagged a trophy just before dark. But it was his first deer, and he didn't know how to clean it. So Meister went out to lend a hand in the twilight. The two men got the deer back home, but Meister then discovered that he had lost a trusty Zippo lighter he had owned for 15 years.

The next morning, Meister went back to the area where the deer had been shot, but had no luck in finding the lighter; he did note, however, that a bear apparently came by in the night and buried the remnants that had been left when the deer was cleaned. He figured the bear must have knocked the Zippo somewhere, so he shrugged off his loss.

A few days later, Meister told a friend, Skip Durant, about what had happened. The following week, Durant called, telling an elated Meister he had found the lighter—a mile from where it had been lost.

"I asked him how that could be, and he told me he had shot a bear," Meister explained. "And when he cleaned the bear, out popped my lighter."

Meister said the bear had to have eaten what was left of the deer and swallowed the Zippo—which lit up promptly when he tried it—in the process.

So does Meister still carry the lighter when he goes out? "Oh sure," he said. "If I lose it again, Skip will find it for me."

Becoming Bowhunters

by Dean Brittenham
Garwin, Iowa

My brother and I come from a family with an extensive hunting history. We have hunted most of our lives, and have had our ups and downs like any other hunters. A couple of years ago, we decided to expand our horizons by becoming bowhunters.

We both read all the material we could gather on bowhunting and watched numerous videos. Many of the techniques we learned we would attempt to repeat in the field. Normally, our plan for hunting white-tailed deer had been limited to treestand hunting. However, my brother had read several articles relating to still-hunting and stalking deer.

Being realistic of my own limitations, I tried, failed and gave up on this type of hunting. I obviously don't have the patience required to slowly stalk through the woods. My brother, on the other hand, thought he was quite the woodsman and continued to attempt to still-hunt and stalk with his bow. He had experienced several close encounters, but they always ended up with the deer figuring out what was going on and leaving in a hurry before he could release an arrow. I chided him on his lack of success, but he persisted in his quest to successfully stalk, still-hunt and harvest a deer with his bow.

We had both harvested deer during the 1997 bowhunting season through special herd management hunts held around the state. These deer were harvested from treestands. During the final week of the 1997-98 late bowhunting deer season, we decided to hunt together to fill our remaining tags. My brother had located a new hunting site for us to hunt, and had spent the past couple of days scouting the area. During his scouting he had surprised a huge eight-point buck, which had been startled by his presence but had slowly walked away instead of running. Since he didn't have his bow with him, my brother could only watch as the deer slowly walked into the woods.

I set up my stand with great anticipation of getting a chance to see or harvest this magnificent buck. My brother decided to forgo his tree-stand, electing instead to attempt still-hunting and stalking. After I had been sitting on stand for over an hour with no activity, I saw my brother coming back toward me at top speed. He was obviously very excited about something, and I thought it must be because he had harvested a nice buck. At any rate, when he arrived at my treestand, he related the story of his successful stalk.

He had quietly and slowly stalked to a heavily used deer trail about 50 yards from my stand. As he was still-hunting, he happened to see large tines just above a small bush. He continued to still-hunt forward, and soon found that he had located a huge sleeping buck. He stalked closer and closer to the buck, who appeared to be oblivious to his presence. He said that he considered shooting the resting deer when he was 20 yards away from it, but the stalk was going so successfully that he decided to see just how close he could get. When he got to 15 yards, he felt that he could wait no longer and quickly drew and launched his arrow. It had been a perfect shot, placed directly into the heart.

As he finished his story, we came upon his trophy. It was a typical eight-point buck with massive 12-inch tines and a huge spread. It was the largest buck I had ever seen in the wild, and would surely qualify as a Pope and Young trophy entry. He ended his story by saying that he had so precisely hit the deer that it had never even gotten up but had died instantly. Having hunted deer all my life with firearms, I knew that even a well-placed shot with a bullet rarely ever results in instant death of the deer. I became suspicious, but how could I deny the effectiveness of his shot with the proof laying directly below me. At this point, my brother began to laugh at me and told me to raise the front leg of the deer to examine the entrance wound. As I raised the leg, it appeared to be very stiff, much more rigid than a dead deer should have been after only being dead for a half hour!

After further examination of the deer, I found the entrance wound in the rear quarter of the deer from a poorly placed shotgun slug. Apparently the deer had been injured during the shotgun season, which had ended over a week ago. My brother's first successful still-hunt stalk had been on a very dead deer! Apparently, this was the same deer he had seen while scouting, which explained why the deer had not run when he had surprised it. The deer must have expired within the two days since he had scouted the area. Unfortunately, the meat had begun to spoil in the unusually warm 50-degree Iowa weather, and we were unable to salvage any meat from the deer. We did, however, harvest a story that we will be able to retell to family and friends for years to come!

Lucky Mountain Goater

by Benton Christensen
Preston, Idaho

S ome call me "Lucky." Others call me something else. I just figured the short wait for a mountain goat tag offset the long wait for my moose tag. Whatever the reason, my 1997 hunting season would be like nothing I had ever experienced.

I have never been a well-traveled hunter, always staying close to a warm meal and a comfortable bed. This year would be different. I had drawn a tag in southern Idaho's unit 67, east of Palisades Reservoir. I had applied for a tag in that unit simply because it was the closest area to home to hunt goats. I had never been in this area before and I knew that I would have to do some serious scouting. After talking to a few people that had been in the area, the name of one place kept coming up: Hell Hole. Yes, it was even on the map. What kind of place deserved a name like that? I was about to find out the hard way.

I had started an exercise program when I received my tag in the mail the last part of May, and by the middle of August I was ready for the first trip into Hell Hole. Two friends from Utah were in search of some "big buck" country and they would accompany me. We soon found out that the shortest route isn't always the easiest. After we left the main trail along Big Elk Creek, the climb soon became so steep that in many places we were on all fours, picking our way up to a series of never-ending ridges. Just when we thought we were at the top, another ridge would appear above us. Finally, Steve motioned to me to join him. We peeked over the last row of jagged rocks into a basin with a green bench at the base of a towering peak, surrounded by vertical cliffs on three sides. There, on the bench, stood a group of about twenty goats. Terrell pointed to another group up the hill a little farther, and suggested that we get closer for some pictures. I was awestruck. In my mind, I thought a group of five goats would be a big herd. As we snapped a few pictures, more goats were filtering in and soon the bench held about 45 animals. We were amazed at the scene in front of us. There were several smaller groups scattered about above and below the main group, and my count soon reached 67. We moved down the ridge to find a suitable spot to spend the night. As we ate supper and made ready for the night, we watched the goats and spent some time glassing for deer along the high ridges. At daybreak, we quickly packed our gear and watched as the clouds moved in. As we started down the steep slope toward the trail, a light rain soon made the descent a slippery and painful ordeal. By the time we made it to the trail, I had fallen several times and I vowed to find an easier way in.

Upon my return home, I hit the phone, learning that there was a good trail into the area in the next drainage to the north. A busy work schedule prevented another scouting trip, so I made plans for my first hunting trip the second weekend of the season. Two days before we were to leave, my hunting partner decided he wanted to hunt elk more than he wanted to accompany me after a goat. I frantically began to call everyone I knew, trying to find someone to go with me. You would have thought I had the plague. Elk fever had control over everyone, and I thought about postponing the hunt until next weekend. However, I had scheduled some time off at work and I decided to pack in a camp and look around a little because I would be going in from a different direction. Over some serious objections from my wife, I loaded my truck and set out.

I have always been a "foot soldier," and my few experiences with horses have been less than memorable. But as I climbed the trail with my camp loaded on my back, I started to go over in my mind the positive aspects of horse ownership. I finally reached a small meadow just below Mt. Baird, which sits at the top of Hell Hole. I looked at my map to orient myself, set up my camp and ate supper. I climbed to the ridge to look around just before dark, and I immediately spotted a big billy. In my haste to beat the fading light, I spooked another goat that ruined my stalk on the big billy. I hurried back to camp in the dark and spent a restless night in my tent. I told my wife that I would come out early the next day, so after looking at some goats on a far ridge early the next morning, I secured my camp and headed back down the trail. Although I felt like I was in good shape, this was still a very rough trip. From the trailhead to my camp, the trail covered over four miles and gained four thousand feet in elevation. Let me tell you, that is a long walk.

I guess this was a way to find out who my friends were. The standard response to my plea for a companion for the next weekend was, "wait until after archery season." Well, I wasn't going to wait. The fear of waiting and then being caught in there by an early snow storm overrode any common sense that would suggest I not hunt by myself. I borrowed a cellular phone from a friend at work and headed out. The drive over and the walk in took most of the day, and I got to camp just in time to crawl into my tent as an unbelievable thunderstorm came crashing in. The storm lasted all night, and, needless to say, I didn't sleep at all. At dawn, the wind subsided and I looked

53

out of my tent into the thickest fog I had ever seen. I ate breakfast and got my gear ready. I thought the best approach would be to get on the ridge and walk around to where I had seen the group of goats the weekend before. Even though the fog was thick, I knew if I stayed on the ridge I couldn't get lost. I worked my way along the knife-like ridge with cliffs on both sides that dropped into an endless fog. I hoped that the weather would break by the time I got to the point where the goats had been. About the time I reached the end of the ridge, a breeze began to blow and the fog began to break up. I quickly spotted a nanny and kid below me. A little more glassing showed another single goat in a spot I couldn't approach. I turned and looked back in the direction of camp. Twelve goats were feeding along the ridge. As I watched them, it became apparent that they were working their way toward me. I excitedly watched as they moved closer, eventually losing sight of them on a curve in the ridge. I began a slow, methodical stalk up the ridge. With a moderate cross-wind to cover my scent and sound, I knew a close encounter was imminent.

I'll be the first to admit that buck fever hits me hard. It was never more evident than now. My high-tech range finder shook in my hands as I tried to get a reading on the goat that stood in front of me. The darn thing wouldn't work. The more I hit the button, the more I shook. After about ten tries, I finally got a reading. I quickly put away my range finder and nocked an arrow. Just then, I could hear a goat walking toward me. I drew my Hoyt Stratus and watched in disbelief as it appeared at five short yards. It stopped with a small bush shielding its vitals. I couldn't do anything but wait. It slowly stepped forward and turned its head to look at me. I don't know why I didn't shoot, but as my finger started to squeeze, I noticed movement underneath the long-horned nanny. She had a kid with her. Time froze as I stood there shaking, and finally I could hold no longer. I tried to let down slowly, but at my first movement, she whirled and disappeared back into the dip she'd come from. Without thinking, I drew again and stepped out to shoot at the first goat I had seen. I could then see several other goats that were closer, but with a few kids in the group, I knew that the only safe shot was at the farthest goat that I had used the range finder on earlier. The other animals didn't know I was there, and a strange calmness came over me as my arrow found the goat.

Even though I had heard and read many stories about this animal's tendency for falling off cliffs, I don't think I was ready for what happened next. I tried to get to where I could see down the chute where it had fallen, and quickly realized that things were not going to be good. There was a long vertical drop onto a steep shale slope. I knew my goat was down there, but I couldn't see it. I made an excited phone call to my wife, and then made arrangements for a friend to meet me at camp the next day.

I knew I was in for a long afternoon. The only way I could see to get down into the canyon to my goat was to get to a trail straight across the drainage from me. I would have to follow the ridge around the top of the basin to get to it. Some three hours later I finally spotted my goat at the bottom of the shale slope. I was heartbroken to see it was missing a horn and had several tears in the skin on its face. With only a little daylight left, I scrambled up the slope looking for the missing horn. I made it to the base of the cliff and slowly worked my way down again, but I just couldn't find it. The job of caping and boning took until dark. As the moon rose, I shouldered my pack and started the long trip back to camp. As I topped the last peak before dropping into camp, I could see the bright lights of Jackson Hole, Wyoming.

I had everything ready to go when Curt arrived the next morning, so we loaded up for the trip out. All the walking had taken a toll on my feet and I could hardly walk when we finally reached the end of the trail. I removed my shoes and my toes were all swollen and purple. Even though my "unicorn" nanny wouldn't make any record book, I truly felt like I had earned this animal.

Later, as my toenails fell off, I lined them up on a shelf in my basement. And I thought: I can't wait. Now I can apply for a bighorn tag!

Belly Laugh of the Forest Gods

by Richilde Glennon
Bennington, Vermont

It was the season of 1996 and I was still-hunting in an area not far from home. I hadn't hunted this particular stretch of woods for a couple of years and was surprised at the changes. I was working my way toward the back end of a corn field. I sloshed through a swamp that now seemed more like a lake due to a family of beavers who moved into the area. After I cleared the swamp, I fought my way through a nasty stretch of briars.

At last, I found a familiar trail, but it was blocked by a large pine tree that had fallen some time between my last visit and now.

There was no getting around the huge tree due to the people-sucking muck that lined both sides of the trail. This was no small tree, mind you. My decision to climb up over its huge trunk was not a quick one, but I took on the challenge. Grabbing onto the dead branches to pull myself over was no small chore. By the time I wrestled myself to the other side, I was sure that any deer within earshot was well out of the neighborhood. By now, I figured that the least I could do was some scouting, since I went through so much trouble to get to where I was. I had just entered an oak stand that lay between the swamp and the corn field when I spotted a chipmunk. It was standing on its hind legs, looking up at me. I thought of how cute it looked and watched the little woodland rodent for a minute or two. I soon tired of that and took a step forward.

The woods around me exploded with thundering hooves. White

flags were flying past me left and right. I had walked right into a herd of deer. I was sure I had scared them all out, when I looked up the trail and saw a couple of does walking right toward me. I stepped behind a small pine tree. I couldn't believe it! After all these years of unfilled tags, I might just have a chance. The larger of the two deer turned and stood on the other side of the pine tree I was using for cover. I drew my bow. Just a couple more steps and she'd be clear of the pine, and I'd have the perfect shot. I swear the forest gods let out the biggest belly laugh that day because what had to be the last surviving mosquito in the northeast came from nowhere and began to attack my aiming eye. I blinked and puffed at the darn thing, but it was determined to suck out my eye. I slowly let down my bow to free up a hand so I could smack the bloodsucker. My movements were spotted by a deer that had been lurking somewhere behind me. It let out a blood curdling snort-wheeze that sent me into the air and my big doe to parts unknown.

Needless to say, I decided to call it a day. As I walked out of the woods, I thought about how my husband and hunting buddies would react to my latest tale of woe.

Eye-To-Eye

by David Hoke
Cedar Hill, Missouri

I was terrified. My first bear hunt and there I was, a thousand miles from home, in a treestand, nervously staring in the face of a ferocious 200-pound bear who had just decided that he and I weren't compatible.

But how could I blame him? Just 18 seconds before, he had begun hugging his way up my tree, and I had whizzed an Easton XX75 over his shoulders in an attempt at bagging the hefty black.

I'm a whitetail hunter, the biggest game of choice back home in Missouri—and I've taken my share of nice deer. I've also made some fine shots directly into the heart of oak trees due to the animal's elusive nature. However, on those occasions when I've missed a nice buck, rarely did it seek the kind of revenge like this Canadian black was apparently after.

It wasn't supposed to be like this. There was no disclaimer in the picturesque, "Happy Hunter With Dead Bear" brochure that read WARNING: Shoot at your own risk. Missed attempts are just cause for retaliation by a respective target. There were some good tips to keep in mind, such as one that dared to suggest I couldn't out-run a bear, and another that warned that while attacks on humans are rare, black bear have been known to attack if threatened or provoked. But there was nothing, not a single word about bears being able to sense the origin of an arrow and subsequently haul butt up a tree to seek and destroy!

My immediate predicament would have not made a great cover shot for the colorful brochure. As the bear shimmied up the tree, inching closer to the base of my 15-foot treestand, my wife's suggestion of a family vacation at Disney World instead of Dad's time with the guys in Canada was, for the first time, beginning to sound like a pretty darn good idea. In fact, at that moment, it was a great idea. But this was a ten-day hunting trip the guys and I had planned for a long time. Tony, Randy and I are all avid bow hunters. It's a year-round hobby, or should I say "investment" for us.

But none of us had ever bagged a bear. I, for one, had never even seen a wild bear until this trip. But I was becoming very acquainted with the creatures, particularly with the growling one right below the weathered ¾-inch plywood that separated us.

In the weeks leading up to our mid-September trip, we had studied dozens of bear videos, read as many articles and obtained as much information as we could about our Canadian destination and the black bear. We were ready.

It was 1,000 miles one way to our camp, which was located in Ontario, about three hours north of Toronto. The conversation during the 15-hour trip from St. Louis to Canada was upbeat and full of anticipation as we all envisioned making the perfect kill shot on a large boar—just like we had seen in the videos. We arrived on a Thursday evening, and before we even took one step on Canadian soil, we could tell that this was going to be a great trip. As we made our way down the primitive gravel road to our camp site, an enormous moose crossed our path, and a short time later, a whitetail with a massive rack.

Our first hunt was Friday evening. I sat dead-still for about four hours in my stand that first evening, watching the doughnut-baited clearing until it was dark. My subconscious was extremely active, though. I swore a large stump, which had an uncanny resemblance to a black bear, was inching closer to me every time I looked that direction.

However, when a couple of squirrels perched atop the snag, my hopeful anxiety took a serious hit. I was depressed. Not a sight nor sound of a bear. When I returned to camp, I could see that Tony and Randy were ecstatic.

Both had seen quite a few bears from their respective stands, but held their shots, hoping for a bigger bear. I was the only one in camp who didn't see a bear. I was convinced that I had drawn the bum stand.

After some good-natured ribbing from the guys, which included a brief refresher course on Bear Characteristics 101, we settled in for the night. When I awoke the next morning, it didn't take long for me to realize why bear hunting is so popular. I contend that it's not just the thrill of the kill, but it's got great hours! Bear hunting is a true gift from God.

Prime bear time is in the evening, which means the bear hunter doesn't need to be in the woods before daylight, which means he can stay up all night with his pals, play cards, share some camaraderie and libations, and then crawl out of bed some time around the crack of noon. It doesn't get much better than that.

I was very optimistic as I prepared for my Saturday evening hunt. I took a few practice shots at camp before heading into the bear woods. I had rehearsed my role in this drama, and now all that was needed was for the star of the show to make his appearance. Just some sort of a cameo would do.

As I approached my stand that evening, I heard rustling around the bait site, and then I saw two cubs scamper up a tree some 25 yards ahead of me. I cautiously approached my stand, keeping a close eye on the growling sow about another 20 yards in front of her cubs. This was a thrill for me.

Throughout the evening hunt, the mother and cubs hung around the bait site. Unfortunately, darkness was approaching and I needed to pack my things up and head back to camp. As I stood up to collect my gear, the two cubs hustled up nearby trees as if they had been spooked. Their excitement roused my curiosity, because I was pretty sure that my little bit of movement wasn't what had caused the alarm. I stopped and looked hard to see any movement.

Suddenly, I heard a log snap, and quickly glanced at the bait pile. There it was—the star of the show. The reason I had come to Canada was a mere 20 yards away, and I had a clear shot!

I'm sure my heart stopped pounding at that moment, but the rest of my body took over and the nervous shakes set in. Before I could nock an arrow, the ever-protective sow approached the boar and the two engaged in a fight right before my eyes. I was amazed. During the course of the fight, the boar turned broadside, giving me my first shot opportunity. I drew back on my XI Legend Magnum and again began to shake, but I let fly when my crosshairs were in line with that sweet spot right behind the shoulder.

The arrow flew over the bear's front quarters, pinging and clanking off the rocks about 10 yards behind him. At this point, I was upset with myself for having missed such an easy shot, but the bear, who was already at wits end with the sow didn't take it so well, either. He spotted me in the tree as I rustled to get another arrow out of my quiver. I had hoped to get off a second shot before the bear left the scene. However, he felt no obligation to leave the area. Instead, he made a bee-line for my tree, and before I could get my arrow nocked, he was at the base of my tree, snarling madly.

At this point I began to recollect another tip from the brochure. "Black bear are one of the few types of bear that can climb trees."

61

Unfortunately, the bear must have read the same brochure. By the time I could say, "Down, bear," he was already on his way up the tree. My first thought was to shoot the charging bear, if I could get an angle. But, I thought better of this when I remembered that even if I hit the boar, he wouldn't go down immediately, and my guess was that during those minutes before he took his last breath, he would have been perhaps the meanest bear in the country. My second thought was to go higher. A quick look up and I could see that the nearest limb was unreachable. My next thought was to just act rationally and apologize profusely. My fourth thought was that the guys were never going to believe me, but I'd certainly like the opportunity to tell them, and my final thought was to put myself in a position to react to whatever the bear had to offer.

My crosshairs found their mark
and my arrow flew.

I went with my last thought and unnocked my arrow, clutched it as tight as possible and waited for the ensuing confrontation.

Another good tip I remembered was that bears are more enticed by movement. Worthy advice, but that had me a little unraveled. Should I move to defend myself, or should I stand perfectly still? It didn't matter. This bear was waist-high and within striking distance, and I knew I had to do some quick thinking.

I was eye to eye, looking in the face of danger and I didn't want to be the one to blink. I took my Easton XX75 with a Thunderhead 100 broadhead and with as little movement as possible, firmly poked the bear in the snout, causing him to momentarily halt his climb.

After a couple more jabs, the bear decided I wasn't worth the fight. So he reluctantly backed down the tree. When I realized the immediate danger had passed, I attempted to regain what composure I had left. The bear headed back to the bait pile where once again, the sow charged him and another fight ensued. I nocked my second arrow and instructed myself to calm down, take a deep breath and wait for a good shot.

The bear was once again broadside. My crosshairs found their mark and my arrow flew. This time there was no doubt. A hard thump, and I knew the arrow had made full penetration. What a relief to see the bear lumber off into the dark woods. Soon the sow and her cubs vacated the area, finally allowing me an opportunity to get out of my stand.

A night rainfall prohibited us from tracking the bear that evening, but we found the bear early the next morning. A clean shot through the lungs had felled the 200-pound bear about 20 yards from the point of impact.

As I look back, I realize my confrontation could have been tragic. But in a way that perhaps only a hunter can understand, I feel privileged to have experienced such a once-in-a-lifetime event—and he, not I, blinked.

The Hancock County Deer Rodeo

by Dan Peterson
Britt, Iowa

It all started out easy enough, so I thought. Be at the right place at the right time, take the best shot for a humane kill, and this buck would be mine.

The only problem with this plan was there were two right places in the section I was hunting. The deer had been crossing regularly in the middle of the section, where the two line fences met, and in another place about ¼ mile east in a small washout.

This left two great ambush points and only one me. What better way to start a buddy out on his first deer hunt than to put him in the second-best place I knew of in that section? He'd get a great experience, and I'd have help dragging my deer. The plans were made, and all we had to do was wait for opening day.

Opening day came and, as usual, I wanted to be out on stand early enough that both our hands and feet could be frozen before daybreak. I would drop Jim off on the west side of the section, so he could walk east toward me by the line fences. According to this great plan, Jim would walk ½ mile, I would walk ¼ mile, and we both would have a chance at the buck.

Everything went as planned, even the cold hands and feet. As the sun came up, I could hear the snow crunching as the deer worked their way to Jim. Not exactly what I'd expected, but what a first season for

64

him. A short time later, one single shot rang out.

Having a gut feeling that Jim was standing over that prize ten-point buck by now, I headed back to the truck for a tarp to drag the deer through the snow. Thinking that if I were him, I'd want to gut my first deer without any help at all, I decided to have a cup of coffee and a roll while sitting on the tailgate of the truck.

Halfway through that cup, a friend pulled up and watched the action through his spotting scope.

"Looks like your buddy has a deer down, Pete."

"Yep," I answered. "I figured only one shot meant success."

"No, you don't understand, Pete. He has it down and he's wrestling it, or riding it—I'm not sure."

Not wanting to miss out on this, I left my coffee behind and took off for the line fence. As I got closer, I could hear the words, at first sort of pleading and then changing to a direct order, "Pete, help me. Pete, HELP ME!" and some words trailing off behind that I couldn't quite understand.

As I topped the hill, I could see what he was hollering about. Poor Jim had his legs and arms wrapped around the deer's head and neck, and couldn't get his knife out to save his rear. The deer would get up, make a big lunge, and slam Jim down to the ground again and again. Not a pretty sight.

When I finally got close enough to help, they were both quite tired. Being pretty beat up and not having his wits about him, I didn't dare give Jim my knife. Instead I told him to hold the deer's head back and I would do the dirty deed.

Not knowing that deer have a nerve in their necks that apparently connects to their rear legs, I had my keister in the wrong place. This made it very easy for the deer to insert his rear hoof, along with my long johns and coveralls, into the "exit only" area. I guess he didn't want me in on the fun.

After arguing with Jim for a minute or two, I decided to try again, and this time we were successful.

As they laid there together in the snow (what a Kodak moment), I couldn't help but ask Jim if he only had one shell, or if he just hadn't wanted to waste another one. Once again I heard that string of words I couldn't quite understand. After a short rest period, I told Jim I would be glad to show him how to gut a deer, if he would show me how to ride one.

It turned out Jim's only shot had removed the right antler of the ten-pointer and only knocked it unconscious. When Jim put his gun down and walked up to examine the rack, he grabbed an antler, and the "ride" began.

So ended the Hancock County Deer Rodeo.

Jim has since then shot many deer and, you guessed it, got to ride an eight-pointer again a couple of years later—with four spectators this time. Seems like when you're good, the crowds just keep growing.

Perfect Shot?

by Russell Brooks
Niles, Michigan

One of my favorite hunting stories is about my father. At the time, he had been hunting deer for over 20 years. I was 10 or 12 at the time. The only time he came home from hunting before dark was if he had taken a deer.

One evening he came home well before the usual time. When he walked into the house, he seemed somewhat angry. When asked if he got one, he said he was empty-handed. He then proceeded to tell us what had happened in the woods—a story that he will never forget.

It was about 5:30 p.m. He had been in his blind for almost an hour when a nice eight-point buck came walking his way. Dad slowly drew back his bow, took aim and released the arrow. He watched in awe as the arrow sailed underneath the fine animal. To his amazement, the buck only moved a few steps and stopped, looking the other way. Dad excitedly reached over his shoulder, pulled another arrow from his quiver, adjusted his aim and took the next shot. The arrow headed right for that perfect place behind the front shoulder. He heard a thud as the deer let out a loud snort and ran off. When he walked over to where the deer had been standing, Dad found his arrow lying in front of the tracks. It was the rubber-tipped arrow that he always carried in case an unsuspecting partridge came his way.

To this day, nearly 20 years later, Dad never carries a bird arrow or hunts with a shoulder quiver.

67

A Hunt to Forget

by Otie Kirbinzky
Doniphan, Missouri

It was cold, crisp and absolutely a perfect morning for the opening of rifle season in Colorado. Bill, Lon, Erskine and I were hunting bull elk in an area near Kremling.

I had been on my stand only a short time when I heard three shots from the direction of where Erskine was supposed to be. I waited for another hour and began hunting that direction. I climbed a steep bank and ran into Lon. He agreed that the shots were probably fired by Erskine. Erskine is the best shot that I have ever hunted with. He almost never misses. For him to shoot three times had us both interested. We decided to find him and see what had occurred. We only walked a short distance and a hunter began waving to us from the ridge above us. He motioned for us to come up the lower part of the ridge. The snow was not as deep in this area. After stopping several times to catch our breath, we finally climbed to the top. Waiting for us was Bill. He also had heard the shots and was curious. He had seen Erskine on the other side of the ridge and we followed him down. Sure enough, there was Erskine with a nice 5x5 bull, gutted and ready to travel. Of course, we all had to hear the story immediately. Erskine said he had been going to his stand when he walked up on this herd of elk. They spooked and ran off. He had waited for a time and began working his way toward where he thought they had gone. He was sneaking along when he looked up and there stood four elk. They walked in front of him in single file. It was brushy, and he could not see antlers on any of them until finally the bull raised his head and looked his way. Erskine said he saw the bull at the same time the bull saw him. The bull bolted and ran. Erskine fired and thought the bull went down. The snow was deep and it took him a minute to get to where he could see. He looked, and he saw a bull elk looking at him behind two big fir trees. Again he fired, and the elk disappeared. This time, he waited and tried to see which direction the elk was going, but he saw nothing. He thought, I must have gotten him. He walked to the spot where the elk was, and looked. No elk, but down the ridge stood a bull. Again he fired, and this time he saw the elk drop. At last, Erskine said, I finally hit him.

When he gutted the elk, there were three holes in the chest area. This elk had not wanted to die. We all examined the holes and could not believe that it took three hits to drop the elk. We all commented what a tough bull he was. Now came the hard part. Getting the elk to a road where we could load him on a truck was going to be an ordeal. We like to hang our game and let it cure after skinning. It is easier to do this with the animal in one piece. Therefore, we decided to drag the whole elk as far as we could before cutting him up in pieces. The four of us started dragging this big bull. The snow was about six inches deep and it helped to drag the elk; it slid well as we were going downhill. About halfway down the ridge, my feet slipped out from under me, and I landed on the bull's antlers. One horn penetrated my pants and entered my buttocks. I screamed in pain. The others could not keep from laughing, and Lon said, "This elk is dangerous even after dying." I was not amused. The wound was serious. The horn had penetrated about 1½ inches into my butt. It hurt. I was bleeding and very sore. We had no first aid kit with us. Everything was back at camp. We continued dragging the elk. I helped as much as I could, but walking hurt. We finally got the elk to the bottom and to the road. I was so sore I had trouble getting into the pickup. Each of the others expressed sympathy, but I could see them winking at each other. They thought it was very funny to be gored by a dead elk.

The only antibiotic we had was kerosene. Talk about pain. Again, this brought laughter. I was so sore the next morning, I could barely walk. I decided to stay in camp. I did get up and help the others to leave for their hunt. A big mistake. We had our lights hooked up to our truck battery. I stumbled around to unhook the cables when Erskine slammed the hood down. He did not see me. My hand was smashed. It was the kind of pain that when your heart beats you almost pass out. I could not believe my bad luck. I have never been accident prone, and I am a cautious and careful person. But now I was a mangled mess. My trigger finger was black and swollen, and I could barely walk. It would have been very difficult to hunt in this condition. I began thinking about my family back home. The way my luck was running, it was possible I might never see them again. I decided to stay in camp and heal up. The only ones there were me and the elk that had caused all the problems. As I sat there feeling sorry for myself, a gust of wind made the elk move where he was hanging on the meat pole. As poorly as I felt, I realized I was in a lot better condition than the elk. That put everything in perspective.

Frogging with Tiffany

by Phil Taunton
Emporia, Kansas

Frogging. What a way for the outdoors enthusiast to beat the heat during hot summer nights. In my state, bullfrogs can be legally taken day or night by traditional fishing techniques, dip nets, gigs or bow and arrow. The mighty bullfrog hunter, clad only in cutoffs and old tennis shoes, who stalks his quarry at night and snatches 'em up barehanded, is in for some fun and exciting moments. A good waterproof flashlight and a gunny sack are really all the fancy equipment he needs. Insect repellent and a gallon or two of courage are helpful accessories that may come in handy at times!

Some years ago, while frogs of every sort chirped backup and crickets and cicadas sang melody to the bullfrogs' foghorn bass, my daughter, Tiffany (then six years old) and I decided to leave the comforts of our cabin at Council Grove City Lake to explore the weedy lake shore and hunt bullfrogs. A certain mystique all its own befalls the lake once the sun sets. After sticking the flashlight under my chin a couple of times while growling and chasing the little urchin, we were ready for some serious frog hunting. Grandma said she would allow us to catch her star of the band, only if we agreed to let the frogs go. Their antics and thunderous "baa-rumphs, baa-rumphs" are really entertaining, but there seemed to be fewer of them around anymore. I never did tell her about the big ol' black anaconda!

I would shine the flashlight into the frogs' eyes and Tiffany did a good job of scooping them up with a big dip net. It was quite cumbersome in her little hands. How cumbersome? We were soon to find out!

Having caught and released several bullfrogs, and after watching the small fish and the crawdads of the shallows dart and scurry to escape the light and find cover under the mossy rocks, we decided to return to the cabin. Suddenly came the alarming sound of a frightening hiss originating from under the weeping willow tree. When I flashed the light in that direction, it fell upon a horrendous *eye* levitating above the ground. I had barely regained my composure and was prepared to take the situation in hand when I heard a dull "whomp!" Tiffany had viciously tee-balled that *eye* with the dip net! Her ability to knock the monster out of sight would have made the Babe or Hammering Hank Aaron proud.

The flattened heap emitted a groan and, when I recognized a pair of size 12 tennis shoes sticking out from under the dark green tarp, I knew it would be a long time before I heard the end of this little episode. My father had sneaked out of the cabin while we were exploring the lake and covered up with a tarp he used to protect the riding lawnmower from the elements. He was peeking through a hole in the tarp and that was the floating *eye* my light had fallen upon, and not some alien man-eating monster!

All he could say when we were patching the cut on his head and trying to stop the bleeding was that I deserted Tiffany, leaving my daughter to fend for herself. He said I even jumped in the lake trying to make a getaway! I alibied and tried to explain that I had merely taken a step or two back in order to plan our defense. You know, just in case there were *two* hissing, one-eyed, green mossy-type critters to contend with.

I must admit, though, my pants did get a little wet!

Three Legs

by *John Mastriano*
Ft. Lauderdale, Florida

Some time around 1970, my son and I had a rural newspaper route of about 400 customers in Guilford Connecticut, delivering the New Haven Register. I would start my route about 2 a.m., driving my full-size Chevy Blazer with my son distributing the papers as I drove by the newspaper boxes. One day, about halfway through our route, I spotted a large buck on the side of the road about 100 yards ahead of us. I pointed him out to my son and slowed down so he could get a good look. As we drove by, the buck charged. He hit the passenger side door of my Chevy, and I stepped on the accelerator, swerving to the left to get away from him.

The seven-point buck ran down the side of the Chevy. When I got away from him, I turned back to see if I had hurt him. When I approached with my high beams on, the buck was in the center of the road. He would stand, then fall, stand, then fall, and continued to do this maybe five or six times. I thought I had broken his leg.

He finally got his footing and bolted across the street through a wire fence. I then approached the area where he stood and found that when I pulled away from him, I caught his front leg with the rear bumper of the Chevy and pulled it out of the socket. The leg was on the street, leaving the seven-point buck with only three legs.

I used my CB radio to call the local police to notify them of the accident. When the police arrived, we followed a red swatch of blood through an open field for over 100 yards, over two fences, and through two creeks before it disappeared.

I notified the area customers to be on the lookout for a three-legged buck. I got a call from one customer the day before Thanksgiving that her dogs were acting oddly that evening, and that a deer was behind her barn. I got her permission to get there early the next morning. A friend and I arrived at daybreak to find that the deer had left the spot where he had been sleeping. This was about two weeks after the accident.

I then suggested that we walk the area to check and see if he was still around. Within about 100 feet, he bolted on three legs and was in the air as if he had wings. My friend fired using a lever action rifle. I fired two slugs with my shotgun. He went down, but he did not die. We had to shoot him again.

When we finally got him, we found that the socket where the leg had been pulled out was healing nicely. He had stuck it in mud, which was caked on the wound, helping to make it heal. He was the largest deer I had ever seen. The buck dressed at about 180 pounds.

I donated the deer to the Guilford Sportsman Association with the understanding that I got his remaining three legs and his seven-point rack.

Camouflage: When is it Necessary?

by Thomas Hulen
Tempe, Arizona

On a recent deer hunting trip in the Chiricahua Mountains of southeastern Arizona, a group of deer hunters was sitting around a campfire telling funny stories about mutual friends and past adventures, when Jesse told us about an experience he had some years back while hunting elk near Lake Mary, Arizona.

Jesse had hiked to the top of a hill so he could have a good vantage point to glass the country for an elk to fill his tag. To his surprise, he saw a lone man standing next to a tree, wearing nothing but his underwear and hunting boots. Being a good person, and having concern for the safety of all who venture into the great outdoors, Jesse thought it best to see if the man needed any assistance.

After a short hike, Jesse reached the man, who was greatly relieved to see Jesse. "I was elk hunting and have been lost for some time. I am so glad you found me."

Jesse reassured him by telling him he would help the man find his camp. Before they started back to the man's camp, Jesse just had to ask the man why he was wearing only his underwear and hunting boots.

"Well," said the man, "no one could have seen me if I were wearing my camouflage hunting clothes. I wanted someone to find me!"

Jesse made sure the man was dressed and safely returned to his camp.

My Yukon Experience

by Joseph Arrain
Tracy, California

It was a beautiful day in September when I headed north for my much awaited Yukon moose hunt. This was the climax of several years of saving and planning. I had decided to drive to Watson Lake instead of flying, as the majority of my working career was as a long haul truck driver and I had driven the AlCan Highway many times, but never since it had been paved.

My trip north was flawless—great weather and a few stops on the way to see old friends and past hunting friends. After leaving Dawson Creek, British Columbia, I was on the AlCan and many fond memories were returning. When I arrived in Watson Lake, I got myself a motel and radioed for the hunt. I met with the outfitter to make our plans for the float plane trip into the hunting area.

Now the horror begins. On arrival at the float plane base, I was told we had to wait for four hunters who, as yet, hadn't arrived. It was about 1:00 in the afternoon, so there was plenty of time.

We waited and waited and waited. The pilot told me that we must take off by 4:30 at the very latest to get everyone to their hunting location and him back to his base. Finally they arrived. We threw their gear into the plane and were off the water by 4:35. The temperature was around 50°F.

We landed at the first lake and I was very impressed. It was a trapper's setup, with a nice big main cabin, several other buildings and a boat dock. The trapper worked as a guide for the outfitter during the moose season.

Off again to the next drop-off point. On approach to the lake, there was a cow moose standing in the water. What an encouraging sight! When I saw the accommodations, boy, it was like a hotel in Las Vegas. This was a fishing lodge where the words "roughing it" were not in the brochure description.

Off again to drop me off. Now I was thinking the first place was nice and homey, the second a palace, number three should be a palace, right? As the plane set down and we floated to shore, I saw a makeshift tent made out of three well-worn plastic tarps, 12x14 in size and eight feet high in the center, but my spirits rose when I saw a nice set of moose antlers. My guide, young and inexperienced, was apparently none too happy to be in the bush, but, I told myself, I was there to hunt moose, not to socialize. As darkness fell, I watched the northern lights, and crawled into my sleeping bag to try to get some sleep.

Morning came—beautiful, not too cold, fairly clear and no wind. We had breakfast and went out in the canoe in a quest for the moose of my dreams. Within 10 minutes, the guide had called in a moose off the hillside. My heart pounded, my knees shook. We went ashore and got into position. The bull never showed himself. We called, grunted and waited. We heard a splash, looked around and saw the bull swimming across the lake. Back to the canoe to chase my dream. The moose exited the water and stood on the bank about 60 yards away. I was ready to touch off the 300 Weatherby. Boy, was I ready. My guide said let's hold off, we can do better. After all, this was the first few minutes of the first day. I put the safety back on and watched the big bull move out of range. We canoed around the lake the rest of the morning but did not see any wildlife except a few ducks and birds.

After lunch and a short nap, we were back on the lake in search of our quarry, my magnificent Yukon moose. By three, the wind had come up and we had to head back to camp. Just as we started back, we were covered from head to toe with snow.

As we woke on the second morning, the wind was blowing, the snow was falling and the "tent" was leaking. The order of the day was to stay in camp. Morning three was more of the same.

On the fourth morning, there was no snow, but some wind. By late morning, the wind had died down enough that we could get out on the lake. As we were getting ready to head out, we heard the wail of a cow moose. Again, spirits rose and a bull moose was on my mind. We went in the direction of the moose call, but alas, no luck. There was no bull and no sign of the cow. We hunted the rest of the evening and returned to camp.

By now I was becoming a bit concerned and puzzled about the duties, responsibilities and overall experience of my guide. For all intents and purposes, he did not seem to have his heart in the hunt, which under the ever-increasing hints of bad things to come, greatly concerned me; not only for my chances of a moose, but for my safety as well.

On the fifth day, still no moose. We did see a black wolf, but no chance for a shot from a bouncing canoe. Most of the day we had snow flurries, and of course, wind. Several times we had to stay in a sheltered cove until the wind calmed down.

On morning six, a repeat of wind, snow and no moose. My guide called headquarters and asked for advice. The decision was made to move as soon as a float plane could be flown in. In mid-afternoon we were informed that the plane was on its way, so we should be ready. The plane landed and off we went to land on a river where another guide and hunter were waiting, also two nice moose racks. As we unloaded our gear, to my joy, there was a cabin. With the prospect of a good camp, very little snow and a new guide with more experience and a

78

definitely more professional attitude, things were looking up.

We spent the evening getting acquainted, swapping hunting stories and planning the next day's strategies. The next morning, we got in the jet boat and down river we went in pursuit of the elusive moose. With three pairs of eyes, I told myself, today I would get a moose. No bull moose, but 14 cows and four calves. I was pleased with the sightings and put my dreams off until tomorrow when there would be that trophy bull moose in camp.

With the morning light, the real horror began. The river that had been flowing the day before was now a ribbon of ice, the boat was frozen in and the temperature was 28 degrees *below* zero. We worked for hours getting the boat out of the ice and the outboard unfrozen and running. By then the river had thawed a bit. The guides decided that we could make it upriver to the next campsite and our pick-up point.

It took 3½ hours to go about a mile, and there we were, stuck in the frozen river. The river froze in front of us and in back of us. We made it to a gravel bar and camped for the night with only a can of peaches, a pound of bacon and a loaf of bread for three men and a dog.

The next three days were pure hell. We were cold, hungry, and had no shelter to speak of. We lit signal fires and tried to stay warm and not think about food.

The following morning, the weather was clearing and I heard a chopper off in the distance. At long last, they had found us. About 45 minutes later, and much diligence on the part of the pilot, we were flown to safety.

Regretfully, I never got my moose, but I did make it out alive and the bad experiences are just memories now and won't keep me from trying again.

As a final blow to an already disastrous experience, on the dark, windy, snowy AlCan Highway, a logging truck from the opposite direction blew me and my beloved Suburban off the highway. Again, luck and the good Lord were on my side, as I came through this with only minor injuries, but alas, my Suburban was a total loss.

The Tent Heater

by Steve Wagner
Cheyenne, Wyoming

One fall, my friend Larry and I decided to go deer hunting in the Snowy Range west of Laramie, Wyoming. This was the first of many hunting trips that Larry and I endured. Having loaded up my 1973 Chevy Blazer, we took off from our homes in Cheyenne, Wyoming, and headed toward the mountains, only a 75- to 80-mile drive.

The heater in the Blazer was going full blast, but I still had to stop several times to clear the windshield of ice and let the inside of the truck defrost. There was only lukewarm air coming out of the heater when we were moving, but it got warmer when we stopped.

By the time we reached the mountains, it was 8:00 p.m., and it had snowed eight to ten inches. We were the only vehicle on the road and it was very slow going.

I drove on an old forest service road for about two miles and found a good place to pitch our tent. While maneuvering the truck to park by the campsite, the left front wheel went off the shoulder and the truck slid about three feet in the snow to rest against a tree. You see, I'm stupid. I only had street tires on the truck and wasn't getting any traction in that snow, which was now about a foot deep. After using a hand winch and a piece of fallen tree limb, we were able to free the truck and park it.

We pitched our six-man tent, which actually only fits four people, two if you want to sleep. We blew up our air mattresses, put our sleeping bags down, and I started the tent heater. It was one that I had rented for the weekend, and the type that uses the stubby propane bottles.

It was about 10:00 p.m., the tent was nice and toasty, and we decided to crawl into our sleeping bags and get some shuteye. But before that, a small flap had to be opened for ventilation. I opened the flap and noticed that it had quit snowing. We then went to sleep.

I woke up about an hour later and was freezing. The tent heater was out and I had snow all over me, but Larry was dry and snoring like a big old bear. I got up to light the heater and it wouldn't start. I changed the propane bottle and it started up again. After just a few minutes, it was nice and warm in the tent. I crawled back into the sleeping bag and noticed that my air mattress was flat. I blew it up again, got back into my sleeping bag and went to sleep.

An hour later, I was freezing again, snow was all over me, the air mattress was flat and the tent heater was out again.

To make a long story short, I changed the propane bottle five more times throughout the night, was unable to keep air in the mattress, and froze with the snow coming down directly on me. Larry stayed warm and slept all night.

When we got up for the day to go hunting, it was so cold that I had to start the truck to warm it up so we could get warm. You see, I had used up all the propane. I had used a total of seven 16.4-ounce bottles.

Larry and I went hunting, had no luck in the morning and decided to go into the nearest town to buy more propane because we were going to stay another night. I bought eight more bottles and we headed back to the mountains.

It was about noon when I turned off onto the dirt road where we were camped. The snow had been melting, but that just made things slicker on the dirt road. As I was driving up the rough, bumpy hill, I started losing traction. I gave the truck a little more gas, hit a bump and stopped. I put it in reverse to back up and see what we were hung up on, but the truck wouldn't move. Larry and I got out and saw that I had run up on a stump that was under the snow and the front differential was resting on top of it. The rear wheels, having only street tires, were just spinning and they couldn't grip in the slick, melting snow.

We both cursed a little, found a large dead tree limb and Larry wedged the limb under the back bumper and put his shoulder into the limb. Larry is just a little guy—6' 3" and about 280 pounds—and bad. He lifted the truck forward off the stump.

My Blazer has continuous four-wheel drive, but I dropped it into 4 low anyway and was able to climb the hill and get us back to the camp without any further problems.

Once at our campsite, I put another bottle of propane on the tent heater and noticed, for the first time, that it had a regulator valve on it to control the amount of heat it put out. I started the heater, put it on a lower setting, and Larry and I had lunch and just laid around in the tent for a couple of hours until we went hunting again. The propane didn't run out the whole time.

Larry and I returned after dark that evening, again without any luck, lit the tent heater and had supper. That night, we slept comfortably all night without having to change the propane.

Everything that Larry and I had to endure that weekend was frustrating and maddening, but it was also very funny when it was all said and done. The most frustrating part was that we didn't get our deer and, 12 years later, I still have six extra bottles of propane.

Short Hunt Down a Long Trail

by Shawn Dawson
Great Falls, Montana

At 6:30 a.m. I flicked off my flashlight. It was now light enough to see. I had been walking for two hours in pitch black with nothing but my flashlight and a small, rugged trail to guide me. This elk season opener was finally here! Just another 100 feet and up a small hill lay a large meadow where I had seen all kinds of elk sign the day before.

My heart pounded as I approached the meadow and spotted a bull elk feeding only 75 yards away! I took a steady rest against a tree and placed the crosshairs just behind his left shoulder. I squeezed the trigger-nothing happened! Eventually, you have to take your gun off safety for it to work properly. I don't think it was buck fever. This was an elk, not a deer. I quickly switched my rifle to fire and let off a round. Direct hit! The second round sent the bull crumbling to the frozen ground.

YES! I was elated. If I could still do a cartwheel, I probably would have. My first brow-tined bull, and he was a nice 5x5.

As I began field dressing him, I looked back in the direction of my truck, which was six miles away, and thought, "What did I do?" I finished dressing him and headed back to the truck. I knew my dad had a horse I could use and I'd get this elk out in no time.

I got back to Mom and Dad's house at 10:00 a.m. "I need a horse," I said as I walked into the kitchen. "You got an elk?" Mom asked. I replied with a confident, "Yep!" After a little coaxing, I finally persuaded Dad to go with me.

So, with the horse in the trailer, Dad and I headed back to retrieve my elk.

We reached the trailhead at noon. I had asked Dad to ride Geronimo, the horse, and I would lead the way on foot. He said his back was sore and didn't want to take any chances. "I'll stay here and listen to the ball game on the radio," he said.

I climbed on Geronimo and told Dad I'd be back in a couple of hours.

In a couple of hours, I finally reached the elk. It was 2:00 p.m. as I approached. Geronimo started bucking. I thought, "Great! This is going to go real smoothly." It's pretty hard to pack out an elk on a horse that's afraid of it.

I first tied a rope around the bull's antlers. Geronimo wouldn't get close, so we had about ten feet of rope between us. As the bull's antlers dug into the ground, it reminded me of pulling a 48-foot duck-foot with a two-wheel drive tractor. It doesn't work!

Off with his head ... I mean, the elk's! I cut off his head and left it there. Now we were gaining some ground! We made about a quarter of a mile and Geronimo started getting tired of dragging this headless elk. He refused to go any farther.

I cut the hind quarters off and decided to leave the rest of the elk where it lay. "I'll just throw these hindquarters over Geronimo!" Geronimo said, "No." He kept circling as I tried flinging the quarters over him. It's too bad it wasn't quarter horse season as well, 'cause I could have filled that tag, too. Now it was back to the old dragging scene. After the saddle fell off a couple of times and about a mile later, Geronimo decided he was done. Besides, it was 5:00 p.m. and getting dark.

Geronimo seemed to know we were heading back, because it took him no time to reach the truck. It was now 6:00 p.m. Dad came out to the trailhead and asked, "Where's the elk?" I don't even remember how many cuss words I used when I replied.

As we headed toward home, Dad said, "Your mother probably got dinner ready and is really ticked off."

Little did we know, she had visions of Dad having a heart attack. All she could think about was me dragging the elk a couple of yards and then returning for Dad to drag him. We got to the house at 8:00 p.m. and still no elk.

My brother-in-law, Robby, showed up at the house the following morning at 8:30 a.m., with his dirt bike. He figured we'd be back early—enough time so he and my sister Tonya could go on an afternoon hunt.

Robby, Geronimo and I got to the trailhead at 10:00 a.m. We left Geronimo tied to the horse trailer for decoration. As I climbed on the back of Robby's dirt bike, he asked, "Ready?" He didn't tell me he was Evel Knievel in a previous life.

When we reached the kill site, I was surprised to see that the bull's head was still intact. We tossed the head on back of the bike and headed back toward the rest of the body parts.

When we got to the front shoulders and ribs, we decided to do some sawing and de-boning. Robby took the front shoulders and back straps while I stayed behind to cut the antlers off the skull and completely cape the bull's head out. I had just finished when I heard the roar of Evel Knievil approaching. We loaded the antlers and cape on the bike and away Robby went again. I continued down the trail toward the hindquarters where I had left them the night before. I then cut the quarters in half and loaded one half on Evel's bike. One more trip would have the elk completely out.

The elk was finally loaded in my truck. What a workout!

It was 4:00 p.m. and as we pulled away, I thought to myself, "I can't wait to do this again."

Kevin's Dead Deer

by JoAnn Moskiewicz
Gilman, Wisconsin

Our friend Kevin is in his thirties, and most of his hunting seasons have been successful since he was a kid first starting out. He is not a stand hunter, he likes to keep moving, slowly working his way through swamps, alders and thick grass, many times chasing up deer to other hunters in his group, many times getting his own deer, many times getting his feet wet.

This year was not to be one of his successful years.

Kevin was just going into a small patch of tall grass on the edge of an open field. As soon as he stepped into the area, several does bolted out of the middle and ran across the field. He kept slowly moving through the grass, back and forth, when he saw what he knew to be the hind end of a deer laying in the tall grass right in front of him. He couldn't see any more of the deer, even though it was only five or six feet away from him.

Immediately he sighted his gun on it, not wanting to just fire a shot into a possible dead carcass. But he was ready just in case something jumped up. He stood there for a bit, and when nothing happened, he took two steps to the left. Still nothing happened. So he took two steps to the right. Nothing happened. He thought, what the heck? Then he decided that this had to be a dead deer, so, putting his safety back on, he took hold of the stock and reached out to poke the rump with the barrel of his rifle. He actually touched the rump when out exploded a nice six-point buck, leaving Kevin backpedaling a few steps and almost dropping his gun. All he could do was stand there and watch this wily animal bound away waving his white flag good-bye.

Kevin said that he wasn't being overly quiet at any time, and now knows the deer knew exactly where he was at all times, and just took the chance that this hunter would walk right by him. Kevin's friends just wish they had this on video. It would have to rate right at the top of the charts.

What a lesson when the bucks are wise to us. We can't overlook any possible place that a deer might hide in, and that particular buck learned a lesson that might make him even smarter and harder to get in the coming seasons.

DEER HUNTING ADVENTURES

Deer hunting means different things to different hunters.

We might gather at a cabin or shack in the woods or brush, or on the edge of a swamp. Some might call a nylon tent at timberline or a canvas wall tent in the pines home for a few glorious days.

But every deer camp—even if it's a state of mind at home during deer season—has one thing in common with all other deer camps: stories of the hunt.

And every hunt has a story to go with it, a memory that is weaved year after year by lamplight or the glow of a stove or campfire, there at deer camp ...

Caught with His Pants Down

by Michael Rhicks
Centerville, Pennsylvania

It was a cold December day. My dad, brother and I were hunting a narrow patch of woods, about five square acres. The plan was to bottle up the deer so they would funnel up to the top, to where my dad was to stand at a corner of the woods where he could see two fields. Dad dropped us boys at the bottom, with the plan that I was to go low around a small swamp, while my brother was to wait 15 minutes and then start to push up toward Dad.

As I worked around the swamp, keeping my eyes peeled for deer, just like that, five deer jumped out of the swamp grass. I shouldered my rifle and started scoping them one at a time. Bingo, there he was. I put the crosshairs on his chest and squeezed the trigger. But at the same time, he slipped on the frozen swamp and his head went back. He bolted up through the woods. I picked up the track, and to my surprise, there was blood. I started tracking him. He was headed right to Dad.

I was close to my dad, 50 to 75 yards away, when I heard the bark of his old .300 Savage. I went straight to Dad and was there pretty quickly. When I got there, I had to do a double take. He was trying to get himself together, but his hunting suit was around his ankles and he was working on getting his underwear up.

I said, "What's up? Where is the deer?"

He replied that the deer was laying in the field about 25 yards away. I said to him, "Let me guess, you got excited and had to go."

91

"No," he said, "I was doing my duty and the deer almost ran over me."

"Let me get this straight," I said. "You shot him while going to the bathroom."

"Yes," said Dad, "In fact, I had to stand up, and I exposed myself to anyone looking."

I just shook my head and busted out laughing. As we got to the deer, it was a nice six-point. We examined him and found that Dad had shot him straight away in the back of the neck. It was a super shot, hard enough to make, let alone with your pants down.

Working our way back to the truck, my brother and I were joking and kidding with Dad when I said to him, "By the way, did you ever get your behind wiped?" We all busted out laughing.

Another 40 Days of Lent

by Tom Lenz
Newton, Wisconsin

E ver since the first time I stood in the woods, quiet as a mouse and stiff as an old timber, clutching my bow and expecting to connect with a whitetail, the experience of bowhunting has to be the most addicting habit I've ever picked up in my 37 years of life on this earth of whitetails.

I had my first bowhunting experience when I was 26 years old, and a man who helped me pick up cattle in the morning lent me his bow. You see, I own a cattle trucking business, and we go to farmers in our area and pick up their livestock and haul them to the various markets to be sold. Anyhow, as we drove the countryside from 6:00 a.m. until 9:00 a.m., our eyes scanning the fields and wooded terrain more than watching the road ahead of us. Sad, isn't it? I had been gun hunting for several years, and decided to try my hand at bow hunting, so Kenny said, "Take my bow and give it a try."

So I bought a license, and the following Friday morning, I headed to the woods behind my grandfather's house. I went down to the corner of the woods where there is a small ravine, and stood behind a big oak tree. This was the very same tree where I had shot a five-pointer that field-dressed 175 pounds during the gun season the year before.

It was 5:30 a.m., a beautiful fall morning, and I was as gung-ho as anyone could get. Not an easy task, but I was standing like a church mouse from 5:30 a.m. till 7:45 a.m., when all hell broke loose. I must have been doing a good job, or it would never have happened. I was watching straight ahead when the brush to my right cracked and rustled. All I saw were antlers tramping through the ravine. Talk about a 500-beats-per-minute heart—I had one. All of a sudden, everything was quiet, but so what, I had a six-point buck coming in front of me, headed on an angle to my rear.

When he looked relatively close, I drew back, and let the arrow fly. ZOOM! It flew right over him. He never hesitated, just kept right on walking. Well, I didn't hesitate, either. I reached over my shoulder to the quiver, grabbed another arrow, turned around and was going to shoot, when I was startled by a snort from behind. I looked over my shoulder, and there stood another six-point buck. What could I do but turn around and shoot at him? He must have thought I was a tree with its leaves rustling, because he snorted, stamped his foot about five times and looked at me while all I did was stand there with the bow fully drawn, my legs shaking and rattling and my heart pounding like mad. I knew that I was more nervous than he was when he calmly looked over his shoulder. I released. Perfect—if he had been four feet taller. He bolted over to his brother.

So now what? I know, turn around again. I don't know why, but I looked back over my shoulder, and there stood a four-pointer. I turned around again, took aim, and shot at him. You guessed it, he wasn't tall enough either. He took off and ran by his two partners. So now what? Right! I turned around, reached over my shoulder and grabbed another arrow. I had three beautiful bucks standing in front of me, so I took careful aim at the closest one, which happened to be the four-pointer, and let drive. If it wouldn't have been for a little birch tree, I'd have hit him for sure. The thump of that arrow hitting the tree sent those deer airborne without any more hesitation. It also sent a doe standing 15 feet to the right of me on an airline cruise. That was the first I'd even noticed her. Gee, and she was the closest. Wow! Four shots at three bucks and no meat on the table, but what fun! That was it. I was hooked.

Since then, I've practiced and practiced, and my shooting has improved 100 percent since that first time out. I've gotten a deer the last four years in a row. This year will be my seventh bowhunting season, so four out of six isn't bad. I've never wounded one but I've missed a few. My love for bowhunting must have something to do with the wobbly knees and pounding heart that occur every time I see a deer. I'm a firm believer in only shooting as far as you feel comfortable, and for me that's 20 yards or closer. Some people feel totally at ease at further distances, but to each his own, right?

I am really glad that I was able to share this experience with you, because I know every bowhunter likes to hear of all the goings-on he can. Thanks to my friend for letting me use his bow. Because of him, I'll be able to enjoy the thrill of getting up before the birds, tramping through a dark woods and waiting for the sun to peek through the leaves so I can get a look at that big ol' buck, and maybe this time put some meat on the table.

The Man Who Had No Knife or Rope

by Donald Mashin
Neillsville, Wisconsin

E very year as deer hunting comes around, hunters always get all of their hunting gear together, especially remembering to bring along a knife and rope.

Well, I have a brother-in-law who is a devoted deer hunter like myself, but John always had one big problem. He never has a knife or rope.

So every year, he would make sure he knew where my treestand was, and we would be within yelling distance of one another. If I happened not to be in my treestand, he would walk through the woods and call out, "Donnie! Donnie!" until he found me. I'd ask him, "What's wrong?" And he would say, "I've got a deer down." Then I would know what he was looking for. We would walk back to where his deer was, and as usual, I gave him my knife and rope to use on his deer.

One year for Christmas, we played a joke on him about never having a knife or rope for deer hunting. I went out and bought a child's yellow jump rope and a toy plastic three-piece knife set, one he could tie around his waist, one for his ankle, and a spare in case he lost one.

I wrapped up the present and put it under the Christmas tree. When he saw the present, he got a strange look on his face, because the tag read "To: John, From: Santa." What was even funnier was when he found the jump rope, knife set, and a little poem from Santa:

Dear Mr. John
As you walk out into the woods
In wonder and dismay
You hope this year a great big buck
Will eventually come your way.

All of a sudden your chance is near
You up and aim and fire a deadly shot
The deer turns around and looks in dismay
And then it goes Ker-Plop.

As you hurry to get out of your stand
And go retrieve your prize
You let out a noisy Ya-Hoo cry
At the buck before your eyes.

Your heart is still thumping,
Your hands are still sweating,
You never gave up hope,
Then you stop and realize,
"I have no gol-darn knife or rope!"

As you stand there scratching your head
And wondering, "Now what do I do?"
You look around to see who's near,
And Donnie comes into view.

You yell to him, "I've got one down,
Come over here and see!"
Then you start to think to yourself
"I hope he has a knife and rope
That I can use, Oh please!"

As you stand there looking down
Upon your great big deer,
They ask you where's your knife and rope?
We haven't got all year.
You look at them with a sheepish grin
And thus begin to reply,
"I have no knife, I have no rope,
I cannot tell a lie."
So as the tradition carries on
from year to year and deer to deer
I hope what's in this box will be
Of use to you next year.

Best wishes,
Santa Claus

After his little surprise, he got an even better surprise when he opened another box, which had his real hunting knife inside.

Now he uses his own knife to gut his deer, but I still help him drag them out with his yellow jump rope.

Too Easy

by Domenik Veraldi
Monticello, Maine

During the late 1950s, there was a group of friends that would hunt every year for deer in upstate New York. We always had a good time, whether we got deer or not. In those days, a doe permit was called a party permit, and was issued one permit for four hunters. This permit wasn't easy to get, so we hunted buck, and if we had a party permit, we would use it toward the end of the season.

We had a friend, Tony, who had never been hunting, and we kept asking him to come with us and try it. We finally convinced him, and he agreed to come. He took the Hunter Safety course, which was required in New York, and prepared for the hunt. Having no rifle of his own, he borrowed an old rifle and was ready to go. We, of course, explained all the hunting techniques to him, such as posting and driving, and to identify his target before he shot.

Well, we finally departed for our hunt upstate. There was some snow, and it was quite cold. Tony, being unfamiliar with the territory, was posted on a rock, overlooking a stone wall about 75 feet away. We told him we would pass by on our way back to camp and pick him up.

As Tony sat on the rock watching for deer, it was approaching lunch time. He decided to have a sandwich. As he was eating his sandwich, a six-point buck appeared just behind the rock wall and stood there, looking at him. Tony raised his rifle and fired. The deer went down. We had explained to Tony that if a deer went down, not to rush to it, but wait a few minutes before approaching, in case it should get up again. Tony did just that.

As he was about to get up to check, lo and behold, there was the deer, standing behind the rock wall, looking at him. Well, he assumed that he had missed with the first shot, so he aimed and fired again. He waited again, but this time, nothing happened, so he got up to take a look. He thought he had missed again. When he got to the rock wall, to his surprise, there were two bucks laying dead. A six-pointer and a four-pointer.

We had told him that deer hunting wasn't easy, and not to be disappointed if he did not see or get a deer. He laughed at us and said it was like fishing in a barrel. To this day, we still get a big laugh when we tell the story. By the way, Tony did not deer hunt after that experience. He said it was too easy.

"I Got One!"

by Willard Payzant
Red Wing, Minnesota

In 1962, my wife and I purchased a 40-acre tract just out of Stockholm, Wisconsin, near where the Mississippi River widens out into Lake Pepin. I decided to try out my luck at hunting on "our new property," having scouted it out before the deer season. I asked my wife if she would like to go hunting with me. Previous to that, she had learned to shoot with a 20 gauge bolt action Mossberg, and was quite adept at target shooting.

So, on opening day, just before dawn, I drove her down the highway to the other end of our property, dropped her off and told her to walk slowly through the narrow path to where I would be waiting for her. I no more than returned to my stand when a nice 13-point buck came crashing through the trees and brush, apparently frightened by another hunter in the direction opposite to where my wife was to come. I downed it with two shots and was standing admiring it when she came along. I called out to her, "I got one!" Whereupon she came over, looked at him, and said, "Oh, it's just a dead one!" She thought I had found it lying there, not realizing that they have to be dead if you "got one." That set me off to a good laugh, and I still have to laugh about it when I tell this story. She's a good sport and always laughs too, and says, "Well, I didn't hear the shots, and I figured he had just found it there."

We had it mounted with a full cape, and it hung for many years on our den wall. It is now gone, but the memory and laughs still linger on, and will always be in our minds.

Since that time we and our sons harvested many deer from that patch of ground. It remains one of the best spots in the area, even though we no longer live there, and others are now hunting it. I wonder sometimes if any other young hunters take their wives out in that woods and find a "dead" deer there like mine did!

Deer Hunting in Southwest Texas

by Robert Bradshaw
Mesquite, Texas

I went out to my deer stand one cold December morning. It was about a half-hour before first light. I climbed up into my stand and got everything put in place. I sat down and looked around, but it was too dark to see anything. I kept hearing a noise like a bird scratching on the side of my stand. I hit the side of my stand with my hand a few times and it would stop, but in a minute or so, it would start up again.

By this time it was light, and I could see. As I looked out, I could see a deer at the edge of the trees. It was a doe, and she looked like she had been running all night. She was wet from her head to her tail, and she was all out of breath. As she came out of the trees, a four-point buck appeared beside her. They came out into the open to eat the grass that was around my stand.

As I watched them, I could see another deer just back in the trees, about 50 yards away. I looked at him with my scope, and could see he was a good deer. About five minutes went by, and he also came to the edge of the trees.

I could see he was a good eight-point, a big deer for my area of Texas. I took the safety off my Remington 7mm Mag. and fired. The big eight-point ran for some 20 yards and then down he went. As I looked at the deer from my stand, I could hear that scratching sound once more. About that time a wild-looking furry animal came in the window of my stand. It was hissing and snarling and just about scared the pants right off me. I pulled out the .380 hand gun that was on my side and fired until the gun was out of ammo. I didn't know if I had hit the animal or not, and I climbed out of my stand to see what it was.

I could not find it, so I went to look at my deer. As I walked away and looked back, I saw that the furry animal was on top of my stand. I pulled out my .380 and fired, hitting the animal in the head. Down it came and hit the ground. It was dead. It was a ringtail cat that had almost given me a heart attack. I killed a good eight-point with a 14-inch rack and a ringtail cat all in one hunt. It was a hunt I will never forget.

Quit When You're Ahead—
and While You Still Have One!

by Russell Boers
Appleton, Wisconsin

This story took place almost thirty years ago. Back then, whitetails were far less plentiful and a dedicated slug gun was a new and rare commodity. A treestand generally meant that you were standing on a tree branch. Preparation for the upcoming hunt often meant buying a few slugs for the old rabbit gun and maybe poking a few at a paper plate stuck to a tree somewhere. Nonetheless, deer populations were thinned out each fall here in central Wisconsin, and many of us were quite happy at the end of the traditional nine-day deer season. Those of us lucky enough to get a deer were especially happy.

Jim (names have been changed to protect the guilty) was fortunate in having located a pretty good deer trail on property he had permission to hunt. On opening morning, he ascended to his tree branch and had a seat, having forgone any preseason preparations other than loading up the old pump and climbing up. Before too long, as fate would have it, a nice little buck came tripping merrily down the trail and paused in range. Jim lined up and squeezed one off, almost. What he got was a deafening click as the hammer fell on his heretofore undiscovered broken firing pin. Away went the buck, and so ended day one for Jim.

At work that night (we worked 8 p.m. to 4 a.m. at the local police department on patrol), Jim sought me out with his tale of woe and begged for the loan of my shotgun for the next day. Having not filled my

105

own tag yet, I couldn't oblige, but was able to secure the use of my father's unused pump gun. A standard-for-the-day, 30-inch, full-choke model—just like Jim was used to.

The next morning, back in the tree on the same branch, here comes the same buck (or a very close relative) down the same trail. Alas, poor Jim is a little tired from working all night and is caught off guard. When he sees the buck, he reacts a little too fast and as he touches off a shot, the recoil catches him just enough off balance to launch him off the branch and almost onto the untouched buck, who promptly vacated the area due to falling hunters.

Back at work that evening, a little sore from the fall but no less determined, Jim again begs use of my gun, having become a slight bit shy of the one that pitched him so rudely from the tree. I'd gotten lucky that morning, so the loan was on with the one caution that he use extra care since I knew he hadn't before used a high-tech-for-the-time new Ithaca Model 27 Deerslayer with a Weaver 1.5 power scope on it. He assured me he would be careful and after all, considering his past day's experience, he knew how hard a 12 gauge could kick.

The next morning found Jim at the base of the same tree, the branch having lost some of its appeal, by the same trail. A very cooperative young buck returned on cue, and Jim steadied down for the shot. As he squeezed it off, he saw the slug go wide and the buck take off across a plowed field at the edge of the woods. Running to the edge, Jim, more determined than ever, leaned into the gun and hit the trigger. The recoil brought the scope into intimate contact with Jim's eyebrow and the bridge of his nose. As he told the story that night, when he came to in the next few minutes and picked himself up, he thought he'd been shot until he looked down and found the scope covered in blood and then realized what he'd done. He returned my gun that night after spending considerable time cleaning the mud and the blood off it.

He still didn't have the buck, but to this day carries a fine curved line down the bridge of his nose to remind him of the year the deer nearly got him.

In Pursuit of the Monster Mulie

by Paul Herrold
Marysville, Pennsylvania

It was early in the afternoon and the weather was unusually hot on this mid-October day. The near 90-degree temperature and extremely high humidity made being out on the vast plains of Wyoming almost unbearable.

As the three of us scoped the surrounding plains with our high-powered binoculars, a cool breeze gently flowed through our hair. Rob Henry of Henry's Ranch in Casper, and my hunting guide on this trip, quickly turned to me and said, "Quick, get down!" As I hurried to the ground, I heard Rob whispering to my dad that there was a huge-racked mule deer grazing on some fresh sagebrush just below us. This truly excited me, since bagging a trophy mule deer was the sole reason why my dad and I drove the 31 straight hours from our home in central Pennsylvania.

My dad smiled, shook my hand, and told me good luck as Rob and I slowly and quietly began our journey toward the edge of the ridge in order for me to get a decent shot at this enormous deer. My dad stayed back so that there would be less noise that the deer might hear. Mule deer have very good hearing, and we didn't want to spook this big monster. Luckily, the wind was in our favor.

The edge of the ridge was actually only about fifty yards away, but it seemed as though it was taking an entire lifetime to reach our destination. Rob and I were crawling on our stomachs like two snakes slithering through a grassy field, to stay as close to the ground as possible.

Suddenly, from deep beneath the sage, a jackrabbit startled me as it leapt out just ahead of me. I lay still for a few seconds, trying to push my heart back up out of my stomach, as I suddenly noticed three magnificent hawks soaring by, scanning the magnitude of their undisputed empire, and looking as though to be the three most free-spirited creatures on the face of the earth. I instantly dozed off into another world, where I imagined, if only for a split second, what it would be like to be that free. I as quickly nudged back into reality as Rob gently tapped the brim of my camouflaged cap with his boot. "Let's go!" he said, as I quickly followed behind him toward the edge of the ridge.

Not only was it extremely hot that day, but the light breeze was blowing dirt and dust in my eyes and loose, dried sagebrush over my bare sweaty back. The deep sage that Rob and I were crawling through was also scratching my uncovered arms, leaving long red scratches, some of which were even drawing blood. I was now also beginning to feel a cramp in my left leg, but I endured the excruciating pain, for I knew that a long awaited trophy mule deer would soon be in my sights.

As we painfully inched our way to the edge of the ridge, I could see the deer for the first time. And what an awesome deer it was! I had seen a lot of mule deer on the trip, but none that compared to this one.

I slowly turned back to see my dad kneeling down far off in the distance. As he gave me the thumbs up sign, I excitedly smiled back. He knew that I had a chance at the deer of a lifetime.

As I waited for Rob to tell me what to do, I spotted seven beautiful pronghorn running at full speed across the plain just east of us, approximately 200 yards away. I hoped that whatever spooked them wouldn't scare off the gigantic mulie that stood a mere seventy-five yards away from me.

Just as Rob told me to get the deer in my scope, he suddenly sighted the antlers of another large buck protruding from the sage a mere five feet from the first. He quickly confessed the sighting to me and told me to hold off on shooting the original deer because he believed this deer to be even larger. This was extremely hard for me since I now had the opportunity at a perfect shot, but I followed Rob's instructions.

Almost as instantly as I spotted his antlers, this huge deer stood up from his deep sleep in order to stretch his legs and have some sage for lunch. I couldn't believe my eyes. This deer was indeed much larger than the first, weighing nearly 250 pounds and carrying antlers that reached almost thirty inches in height.

I quickly turned my rifle onto the stag and swiftly put his shoulder in the center of my crosshairs. I did everything just as my dad taught me many years ago. I took a long, deep breath, since my body was shaking and my heart was pounding with excitement, and slowly exhaled while at the same time flipping off the safety of my rifle, hoping that this big buck wouldn't spot us. I gently squeezed the trigger of my Remington .30-06 deer rifle. As I heard the piercing sound of the most devastating of shots ringing across the plain, I knew that the hunt for the "monster mulie" had quickly come to an end.

The Price of a Deer Hunt

by Daryl Jackson
Raeford, North Carolina

It was the end of November and the gun season in Mississippi had opened a few weeks earlier. My brother-in-law and I had decided to make an evening hunt. We had hunted the area before, and each decided where to go. He decided to hunt my stand, which was located in a draw overlooking a creek bottom with a pine thicket on one side and hardwoods on the other. Several nice deer had been seen in the area. I decided to hunt a box stand overlooking a hay field. Late in the evenings, deer would cross the field from one stand of hardwoods to another located on the opposite side. Our locations were around 800 yards apart as the crow flies.

We arrived that evening at approximately 3:00 p.m., knowing that legal shooting hours would end around 5:30 that evening. I climbed into my stand and settled down, not expecting any activity until the last thirty minutes of daylight. I was preoccupied watching a group of gray squirrels playing in the top of an oak tree when I heard a shot ring out from my brother-in-law's direction. I looked at my watch. It was 4:10 p.m. He had been on the stand less than an hour. I remember thinking, I hope he didn't shoot that big buck that I had been seeing off that stand during bow season. I never had him close enough for a shot.

Now, don't think that I'm selfish. It's just that I had been hunting that particular deer and when my brother-in-law asked if he could hunt my stand, I agreed. Hey, he is married to my sister.

With the excitement of the gunshot, I re-focused on the hunt, thinking that possibly the deer were moving early. Maybe half an hour had passed and prime time was fast approaching, when all of a sudden someone started blowing a truck horn in the direction I had parked. Honk! Honk! Honk! The field is only 200 yards off the dirt road. I thought, who is that nut? Well, maybe two minutes had passed and the horn started blowing again, except longer. Honk! Honk! Honk! Honk! I refused to let this horn-honking idiot ruin my hunt and held fast. It didn't work. A short period later, the individual really laid down on the horn and blew it continuously, non-stop, for what seemed like five minutes. I had assumed earlier that it was my brother-in-law, that he had bagged a deer and needed help packing it out. Who else could it have been? No one else knew I was there. I didn't understand why he couldn't wait until after my hunt, but the horn honking made me realize that something was wrong.

I climbed down from the stand and headed for the truck. Halfway to the truck, I saw him coming. I asked, "What is wrong?"

As he got closer, all I could see was blood on his chin and down the front of his shirt. I asked, "What happened?"

He said, "I bit my dang tongue."

I know it's not funny, but with his expression and the slurring of his speech, all I could do was laugh. I realized that he was not seriously injured, and as we walked toward the truck, he began to tell the story with me laughing all the way. It seems that shortly after he climbed into his stand, this monstrous buck walked out of the pine thicket and down the creek bank, right in front of him. He placed the crosshairs right behind the front shoulder and squeezed the trigger. The buck went down, but down into the creek bottom out of sight. Sounds indicated that the deer was trying to climb out of the creek bottom.

My brother-in-law's fear was that the deer may decide to run the length of the creek bottom. He climbed down out of the stand as quickly as possible and started toward where he had seen the deer go down. In his haste, he forgot about a fallen barb-wire fence about a foot off the ground. Just on the other side of the fence was a six-inch sweet gum tree. He tripped on the fence and did not have enough time to prevent taking a big bite of sweet gum. Once he regained his composure and the tweety birds disappeared, he walked to the creek to find his buck lying on the bottom.

By the time he and I pulled that deer out of the creek bottom, it had to have weighted at least one thousand pounds—so it seemed. We returned home, and while he and my sister paid a visit to the local emergency room I skinned out one of the finest eight-points that I had seen in quite some time.

This is not the end of the story. Oh, no. It is my understanding that the nurse at the emergency room got the sutures mixed up. You see, my brother-in-law not only bit his tongue, but also had a small cut on the bottom of his chin. The doctor inadvertently picked up the wrong sutures and began sewing up his tongue. Halfway through the process, the nurse walked back into the room and said, "Doctor, you're using the wrong sutures."

Well, he had to take those back out and start over. By this time, though, my brother-in-law was not feeling any pain and it didn't bother him a bit. He took eleven stitches in his tongue and three in his chin.

When they returned home, even though I couldn't understand a word he said, my sister said that he wanted me to load the deer into the truck and ride with him to take it to the butcher. I really don't think he could find the truck, much less drive. The deer was transported to the butcher the next day, and two weeks later we figured that, after two doctor visits, the butcher bill and other incidentals, the meat was priced at almost ten dollars per pound.

The deer head was mounted and is proudly displayed on his den wall as a reminder. You know, I don't think he talks very plain to this day!

Cold or Bored?

by Norman Abdella
Waterbury, Vermont

My brother, Joe, and I have been hunting the same area for about six years, three of them bowhunting, also. A friend of ours, Brian, wanted to come along to see what it was like. We told him he should take a Hunter Safety course and get warm clothes before he could hunt with us. He agreed it would be great, took the course and did very well at it. He next built a hunting wardrobe, including everything you could think of. We took him out for a trial run on quietness, and he passed.

For bow season, we decided we would sit him in my normal spot. Joe and I went up through the ridges and pushed toward him. The whole season, we pushed deer around the hillside and toward him. Every time we went to meet up with him, he had moved to the truck.

The weather wasn't all that cold, maybe as low as 40°F. When we asked why he kept going to the truck, he said, "I need warmer clothes."

We agreed that we would try pushing again during rifle season, if he would get different clothes.

He got "warmer clothes" and we tried again. Again we pushed deer his way, again he wasn't there. We asked what now, and he replied, "Cold still."

Blackpowder season was our last chance. We sat him again. Again he was not there. We pushed all kinds of deer to him, and kind of blew our season to help make his better.

At the end of the season, we finally asked how come he kept going to the truck. Was he really getting cold, or was he just getting bored? He assured us he would have loved to stay out in the woods, but he really was cold. Joe and I both kind of snickered, and Brian asked what was so funny. By now Joe and I were full-fledged laughing when I finally asked him, "Is it really all that much warmer standing on the side of the road next to a locked truck?"

When Brian realized how foolish it was, he laughed with us and agreed to try harder next year.

114

Ode to a Deer Hunter

by Carly Gustavson (Daughter of Jim Gustavson)
Chippewa Falls, Wisconsin

'Tis early morning he must raise,
To the field in orange of blaze,
To his stand with trusty gun,
He must arrive before the sun.
As the light of day begins to near,
In the distance he sees a deer.
With much tradition and practiced skill,
He prepares himself for the kill.
With steady hand he takes aim,
So there is no suffering for the game,
For he knows if not by the gun,
Mother Nature's job will be done.

The Warmth of a Pasture

by Daniel Foard
Elberton, Georgia

I looked over the most beautiful pasture I had ever seen. The sky was blazing red and purple. I intensely scanned the woodline. My heart was pounding, my breath was visible.

The afternoon before, my hunting partner had taken an impressive nine-pointer. We had found sign that suggested something much larger hiding in the swamp that bordered our newly acquired gold mine of possibility.

Stinging temperatures never crossed my mind. I had positioned myself in the crook of a hill, where I was as warm and comfortable as I would be still at home in my bed. Today was far too important for fidgeting or noise of any kind. Early in the morning, I found the warmest, most comfortable stand in the county.

I patted myself on the back. In 90 minutes, I would be the talk of the county and the envy of hunters across the nation as they gazed upon the photo of my buck antlers spread wide, thick as oak trunks and almost as high. A noise behind me made my heart thump even harder. I was scanning the wrong way, why was he coming from where he never belonged? Louder he came, when I realized it wasn't my buck at all. Kevin, my hunting partner, the one who had taught me how to hunt, was trying to muffle his laughter.

My mind screamed, "What are you doing? Please shut up!" But the choking laughter continued.

Finally, I mouthed, "What's so funny?" The reply came, "Loo-loo-look, y-y-you ..." The squeals came louder this time.

"Shut up," I whispered quite loudly.

"Look behind you!" came the reply, choked through hysterical sobs of now deafening laughter.

Shifting in my seat ever so slightly, still trying to salvage any chance of now seeing my prize, I peered down and behind. I realized that my euphoria over my choice of spots was premature, as I realized that what had kept me so warm all morning was nothing more than a fresh pile of cow dung, steaming and wet.

The tranquillity of the morning erupted in hysterical laughter. The hunt was over.

I was the talk of the county, not as the hero I had imagined, but as the genius who had used the best cover scent of all.

The Monster Buck
of Bully Hollow

by Virgil Puckett
Warren, Ohio

One of the best practical jokes we ever pulled off was for opening day of buck season in the mountains of Pennsylvania.

Every year, everyone eats Thanksgiving dinner and piles into the trucks to get to camp, in spite of all the grumbling wives and relatives watching parades and football on TV after dinner. Opening day is always the Monday after Thanksgiving. They just don't understand that there is a lot of preparation for opening day. There is firewood to cut, and we have to shoot a few rounds through the old trusty rifle to make sure the scope didn't get banged around on the two-hour drive, not to mention having to hunt down and evict the mice that live at camp most of the year.

Well, one particular year, we received a phone call from our old buddy Jimmy. For a reason I forgot, he could not make it to camp until Sunday afternoon, so he asked us if we would find him a good spot to sit for opening day. We agreed.

We knew that Jim liked to hunt down in what is known as Bully Hollow and that he was familiar with it. With a little help from some red survey ribbon, Jim would be able to find the spot that we had picked for him pretty easily in the black of early morning.

After my buddy Ted and I had picked our spots, we headed out early Sunday morning to find Jimmy a spot. After hours of walking, we decided on a spot on a hillside that looked like it would be a good stand for Jim. After building him a great ground blind to sit in, we decided that we should make it really look like the best spot on the mountain to kill a buck. So we got out our hunting knives and picked out about a dozen or so 10- to 12-inch trees and began making some impressive rubs on the trees around his blind, not to mention a couple of impressive scrapes.

Then it was back to camp. After a hot shower and some leftover turkey sandwiches, we heard a truck rumbling up the gravel road. It was Jimmy pulling into camp. He was pumped up, ready for opening day of buck season. He would hardly shut up as he unloaded his gear from the truck. After he got settled in, we told him where his stand was on an old, torn-up topographical map that has stands marked all over it from years of hunting. We told him we almost didn't give him this spot because of all the buck sign there. But because it was so late in the day, we did not have time to go to our blinds and get the gear we had left in our blinds for opening morning.

Opening day came. We didn't see Jimmy all day. Finally, at dark he showed up. The first thing he did was thank us for not taking the best spot he had ever seen in Bully Hollow. He then went on to explain that he had spent the entire day studying the sign around his blind. He said any buck that would rub on a tree that size had to be the biggest buck that ever lived in Bully Hollow. He was so pumped up that no one dared to laugh or even smile, at least while he was in the same room.

For the next three days, as long as there was light in the sky, Jimmy was in his blind in Bully Hollow. He never did kill a buck that season. It was a year before anyone told him. He's never asked us to scout out a blind for him since. But every buck season, someone always has to ask Jimmy, "You seen any big buck rubs lately?"

HUNTING WITH FAMILY & FRIENDS

What would hunting be without the people with whom we hunt?

Anticipation, success, excitement, failure, challenge, cold, heat, wind, snow, rain, plentiful game, no game ... the one constant through it all is that you have thoughtfully chosen your hunting partners. Because sharing the experience with someone you care about makes the memories all the richer ... and last all the longer.

So here's to hunting companions, those classified as family and friends we deem special enough to share a forest, field, marsh or mountain with, creating hunting memories of the best kind ...

Winning the Lottery Twice

by Dan Evert
Fargo, North Dakota

The recollection for me starts in a blur because at 10:15 a.m. on a Thursday, I am supposed to be asleep. After getting off the graveyard shift at 7 a.m., I am scheduled to return to my work in building maintenance at the municipal airport at 2:30 in the afternoon. That makes for a short day's sleep.

That morning, I awoke to a voice coming from somewhere in my sleepy fog. My sweet wife, Bonnie, was coaxing me to pick up the phone. It was my good friend Kevin, ranting about two huge 4x4 bucks with their antlers locked from fighting.

It is rare to find bucks alive in a death-lock. I figured Kevin had slipped up on his blood pressure medication and was having hallucinations. Kevin was on sick leave recovering from a brain aneurysm behind his right eye and the surgery to correct it. Humor him, I figured; get dressed, wake up and listen harder.

Due to the surgery, the doctors had said gun hunting was out of the question. They had even forbidden archery because of the danger of falling from a treestand. Kevin was struggling with equilibrium and judgment difficulties following the surgery.

Kevin is an avid shotgunner. He is in his element on the sporting clay range or hunting roosters in the field. He is equally at home with a .25-06 in his hands during the whitetail harvest. He is no stranger to the compound or recurve bow, and his interests and skills include

123

almost every outdoor sport. Pretty hard to take a doctor prohibiting all the forms of recreation you love.

Kevin called me for help because he knows I work nights, and he was absolutely sure I'd be home. I think he just wanted someone to pull him out if he fell in ... did I mention that the bucks were in a water-filled drainage ditch? Kevin had been out exercising his Labrador retrievers when he spotted something out of the ordinary in the drainage ditch. One look through the field glasses confirmed a pair of huge bucks in a death lock. According to Kevin, one of these locked bucks appeared to be dead. Dispatching the big buck sounded simple enough, but it was not without some heart-stopping moments. We approached the pair of bucks to within 50 yards. Both banks of the ditch were sloping, rain-soaked clay. Now I was beginning to see why Kevin wanted me along. This was a dangerous proposition if you were dealing with balance problems and were out here alone.

Remember now, Kevin hadn't let an arrow fly since before his surgery. His first arrow dropped under the big buck; this is where our hearts stopped. We both witnessed the huge fellow pick up his dead opponent, fling him overhead and slam him down on the offending arrow. That was unnerving. We never found that arrow either.

Kevin decided to use all of his aiming devices this time and looked through his peep-sight while lining up his yardage pin on the big buck. This time the arrow was away and in less than two minutes, the razor-sharp broadhead had done its lethal work. The spirit of the doomed buck was now free.

The taxidermist estimated that the first buck down was 180 pounds, the second was well over 200. He also had to cut an antler off to part the two bucks in order to cape them out. No amount of prying with a length of pipe and two-by-fours could separate them.

So Kevin figured he'd won the lottery twice. Once by surviving the aneurysm in July, and again with his trophy of a lifetime. Not to mention a kidney transplant five years ago. He needs a hat that reads "Lucky!"

Paradise

by Larry Conrad
Kirkland, Washington

My desires to go hunting started at about the age of six. We were visiting my grandparents, and my grandfather took me into his den to show me the most marvelous thing I have ever seen. From his gun cabinet, he removed a Winchester Model 24, 12 gauge shotgun, telling me that this was to be mine. He showed me how to hold the massive weapon. It was so big and heavy that I needed help to hold it up and site down the barrels. I learned how to clean that gun, and on each succeeding visit I would get to retrieve my prize. While running a cleaning patch down the already clean barrels, I would be thrilled with stories of the ducks and geese that had fallen to this wonder of a long gun. By the time I was 10, the gun had been moved to my parents' house and was put away in my dad's closet, still waiting for the time when I would get the chance to follow in the footsteps of my grandfather and bring freshly harvested waterfowl to the dinner table.

My chance finally came during the fall of my 12th year. Together with my best friend, Gary, and both our fathers, we were allowed to go duck hunting. Since the double-barrel Winchester was still too big for me to properly mount into a shooting position, I would be using a single-shot .410 that my father had received as a youth. On the morning of that fateful day, Gary and I were eager to get going; the smell of fresh coffee and Hoppe's No. 9 filled the clubhouse of the hunting club our fathers had gotten permission to hunt. In borrowed hip boots that were several sizes too large, I started out across flooded fields as we headed to our assigned duck

blinds. As the fields were farmed every year, they were plowed and plant-
ed. Walking across the plowed rows proved to be extremely difficult for
two 12-year-old beginners. Soon we were both completely wet and our
waders were full, as we kept tripping and falling while crossing that field.
Both of us ended up giving our shotguns and equipment to our fathers to
carry, and we took off the much too large boots and, for all intents and
purposes, swam to the duck blinds. Fortunately for us, it was a warm fall
day, and once the sun was up and the ducks began flying, all thoughts of
being cold and wet left us.

I don't remember if I actually hit anything, but I do remember walking back to the clubhouse carrying the day's bag. Once back at the clubhouse, sitting in front of a fireplace, drinking hot coffee and drying out our
pants and shirts, I knew for certain I had found paradise. Gary and I spent
the next several years hunting together with our fathers and their friends.

I did finally get to carry and use that Winchester model 24. It still holds a place of honor and respect in my gun cabinet, and will be passed on to one of my sons, all of whom have been introduced to hunting themselves. Each of their first trips was much drier than mine was, but I do hope that it was as memorable. My wife doesn't understand how we can be happy to go out during a fall storm and sit in a blind in the wind and rain and have the time of our lives, then come home on a bright, sunny day and complain about the "bluebird weather." But then, she had no desire to swim to a duck blind as a 12-year-old kid and marvel at the sound of a duck call, or see the beauty of a well-trained dog hitting the water as he is sent on a retrieve. Yes, even today, almost 40 years after that fall swim, each year I again believe that I am seeing a little bit of paradise from a well-dressed duck blind. I now am entering a new period in my life. I am looking forward to the time when I can introduce my own grandchildren to the sport of hunting. I have enjoyed the company of each of my sons in the field, and we have many stories and tales to tell and share. But I think there is a special bond between a grandfather and his grandson. Maybe it will be a grandson who will receive that old Winchester. I do know a couple of young fathers that would be a little disappointed, but if it would help pass on the hunting tradition, I am sure they will understand.

Like Father, Like Son

by Tom Danks
Roy, Utah

This is one of those stories that is only funny now that a good deal of time has passed. I had all but given up hunting while I was going to college, and since graduation had only thought about hunting. So when my fifteen-year-old son started taking hunter safety classes, I started "thinking" about it a lot. Well, we started going to the range, and I quickly got back into the swing of things. My son turned out to be a pretty good shot himself (he must get it from his mother), but this would prove to be worthless during the upcoming deer hunt.

Before we knew it, the hunt was on. We had a pretty active opening day, but saw no antlers. As we were making our way back to camp, the sun had dipped behind the mountains but it was still light enough to hunt. We had pretty much written off the day as a hunt, and were just gabbing and joking as we slowly walked. As we came over the crest of a hill, the terrain opened up to a large, flat meadow, stretching out about 250 yards. Suddenly, below us, a movement caught my eye. Two deer were moving out onto the meadow. They were about 60 yards below us, and were in shadows. I quickly grabbed my binoculars and spotted a good-sized two-point, following a bigger doe. I called to my son, "Take the shot." (Now, remember, it had been a very long time since I had been in this kind of position). I called to him again, "TAKE THE SHOT," but I heard only the sound of my heart, which had started to pound like a drum. By this time, the deer were about 80 to 90 yards out, just about the limit of my son's 30/30. Finally, after what seemed to be an eternity, he called back, "I can't." As it turned out, what we had failed to practice was target acquisition using a scope. So it was time for me to step up and fill my tag. The deer were about 100, maybe 125 yards out. An easy shot for my .300 Win. Mag. (I must interject here that my shooting skills are a combination of what my father, my uncle and the U.S. military have taught me, all of which went right out the window at a time when I could have used them the most.) On my first shot, I jerked the trigger, and as expected, shot wide. I figured all I needed to do was sit down and brace myself. I moved down the hill about 10 yards and sat down. The deer were about 175 yards out, and my heart was in my throat. I shot again; missed. The adrenaline was starting to kick in and my heart was pounding so hard that each beat was being telegraphed into my scope. At about 200 yards, the deer that had been moving away from us shifted directions and began moving across the meadow, giving me the most perfect profile to shoot at. The exhilaration of the moment was only compounded by the sweat dripping into my eyes. I was breathing so hard I could barely hold my Ruger steady enough to aim. I took my third shot. This one was close enough to make the buck stop running, but not close enough to even break skin or ruffle fur. I now had one shot left. The deer were heading for a grove of trees at the edge of the meadow, and they were at a full run. In retrospect, if not for gravity, I couldn't have hit the ground. I tried to squeeze the shot off, but alas, all I got for my efforts was a wave from the buck's puffy tail as he moved into the grove of trees and over the ridge.

One would think that this would be enough of a story to end it here. But after much jeering and finger pointing, my son and I made it back to our camp. As I was taught, and as I have taught my son, we stopped to unload our weapons before we entered the camp. As I emptied my gun, I looked over to observe my son unloading his rifle. I noticed a peculiar look on his face. As it turns out, in his early morning zeal to get afield, he had failed to place a round in the chamber after loading his Winchester. It was now my turn to do some finger pointing.

Overall, the hunt was not a bad one. We didn't get the deer, but we did get a pretty good story. Even if it was the kind of story that only a father and a son would find amusing.

My—Make that Our—
First Grouse

by Christopher Daniels
Clear Brook, Virginia

Penn's woods were alive that cool, crisp November morning. The squirrels rustled in the frost-covered leaves, searching frantically for yet another acorn to tide them over through the winter. Our equally noisy intrusion was greeted by the loud squawks of a sassy blue jay.

Dad had been promising to take me grouse hunting. Small game season was nearing an end, and still I had not bagged my first grouse. Overtime at work had kept Dad from his promise until now.

A fresh carpeting of leaves made sneaking impossible that morning. At best, the two of us sounded like a cow walking through the woods. But still, much like the squirrels, we found the cool air invigorating, and pressed on.

As we crossed a creek and headed up a hollow, Dad stopped suddenly. "Did you hear that?" he said.

"Hear what?" I replied, with the sound of rustling leaves still ringing in my ears.

"It was a grouse drumming—" he said, and then he paused suddenly and listened. "There it is again."

The only thing I could hear was what sounded like someone trying to start a lawnmower off in the distance. After a few more drums and me still not making the connection, Dad explained that I was hearing not a lawnmower, but the sound of a drumming grouse.

131

As with most 15-year-olds fortunate enough to grow up in Penn's woods, I regarded my father as the greatest sportsman ever. Today, more than 15 years later, I still feel the same way. He unselfishly shared a lifetime of information about hunting with me. Even more importantly, he taught me to respect all of nature's invaluable creations. Dad never killed anything just for the sake of killing. He always made use of the hide or the meat. I only saw one exception to this—a groundhog. He had read an article about how delicious groundhog was, so he decided to try one. He went out hunting and shortly brought home a young, plump groundhog. We started to skin it, and the smell was so bad that he very quickly gave up on groundhog fillets.

But our quarry today, the elusive grouse, was an indisputable delicacy. A delicacy that, unfortunately, rarely crossed our table. Bagging a groundhog was one thing, but bagging a grouse was an entirely different story. I had successfully connected on two whitetail bucks in previous seasons, and even a turkey, but the quick, wary grouse had eluded me.

Flushing a grouse was not the problem. It was almost predictable. Any time I was wading through brush up to my ears or paused to remove a greenbriar that had attached itself to my inner thigh, a grouse would flush. I have since learned that those pauses are a key element of successful grouse hunting. Now, I strategically pause so that I have a somewhat unobstructed view of what is ahead.

But this day was turning out to be uneventful. We had been in the woods for about an hour without a single flush. A little cabin that we used for camp during the deer season stood ahead. An outhouse had been built over the summer, and Dad decided to put it to good use, even though no one had gotten around to putting a door on it yet. While Dad was in the outhouse, I was busy kicking the bushes in hopes of flushing a grouse. Suddenly, one burst out of the brush like a rocket, and my old single-shot 20 gauge cracked. The grouse immediately went down but hit the ground running. I had only winged it. The grouse may have escaped if it had not made one fatal mistake. The escape route it chose took it right in front of the outhouse. My dad, who was sitting inside listening to the ruckus, shouldered his shotgun and finished off the grouse as it ran by.

So, with the help of Dad, I finally got my first grouse. It was a handsome bird, and I still have the tail feathers today, all these years later, neatly pressed in an old Sears catalog. By the way, we never did get around to putting a door on that outhouse.

Never Quit

by Mark Prater
Wenatchee, Washington

I am the oldest of five brothers. As you can imagine, we spent much of our youths afield. Dad was a great teacher of the outdoors, and his commitment to hunting was easily passed down to us. We were always in pursuit of some elusive game.

For each of us the thrill of the hunt was for a different reason. My third brother, Reed, was the one who would never quit. He used to test us all during the Christmas holidays by hunting every day for weeks on end. We all love to hunt, but with four boys in their teens, there wasn't enough time to hunt all day, chase girls all night and maintain a proper level of sleep. This guy was persistent. During his senior year in high school, Reed sustained a career-ending football injury. Now this was a true shame, for Reed had a natural ability to have continued his passion for football to the collegiate level. Normally you would think that an individual with his right leg in a cast would have given up the thought of hunting for the year. Not Reed. Shortly after the injury happened, my brothers, Dad and I went on our November elk hunt. We knew things would be slightly different this year. I mean, how far could a guy go on crutches anyway?

Once we took care of the camp chores, we decided to plan the opening hunt for the next morning. Reed was bound and determined not to be left out. Neal, Matt and I were going to hunt the upper portion of one of our favorite ridges. Reed and Dad were going to park

134

down below in the event that any elk might get pushed toward them. I was feeling very confident about the opener.

The alarm clock sounded loudly at 4:00 a.m. We all jumped out of bed, scarfed down some grub and headed out to our prearranged destinations. Neal, Matt and I had to travel some distance before bailing off the ridge. We soon split up, and agreed to meet some time after noon to discuss our findings. I was going to be on the farthest ridge over, which, if my calculations were correct, would place me on the ridge just west of where Dad and Reed were to be viewing from the bottom. As I was making my way across the last heavily timbered area before breaking onto the ridge line, I realized that I hadn't allowed myself as much time as I would have liked. I just started to climb up the final ridge when suddenly I saw movement. I could tell right away that another hunter had beat me to the location. It was too late to backtrack and I thought it best to inform the hunter of my two brothers' whereabouts, so I continued on up the hill. As I approached, I could see this aging veteran hunter looked somewhat puzzled. I introduced myself and explained the locations of Neal and Matt. The gentleman appeared as if he wanted to talk a little, so rather than run off, I leaned against a big fir tree and listened to what he had to say.

He told me he had started very early from a place I didn't even know existed, in hopes of having the mountain to himself. As it started to get light, he had heard something. I was sure he was going to tell me that I had sounded like a herd of elephants making my way through the timber in the dark, but this wasn't the case. He said the sound was almost like metal clanging. He also said he could hear grunts like a bear or pig or something along those lines. He noted that the sounds would go on for a minute and then there would be nothing. This continued for quite a while until finally he could see where the noise was coming from. He looked at me with that wrinkly face and, slightly moving his head from side to side, said, "In my sixty-five years of hunting, I have never seen the likes of this."

I was not sure what he was talking about, so I encouraged him to continue.

"When I first heard those noises, I was sure it was a herd of elk. Then I thought it might be a bear, but I couldn't figure out the clanging. When I finally saw movement and realized what I was looking at, I just couldn't believe my eyes. There, on the opposing ridge, was the craziest hunter I have ever seen. This guy was lying flat on his belly working his way up the crest of the ridge. I couldn't make out what looked so odd at first, but then I saw what he was doing. He would push himself up the hill about a body length, then throw a pair of crutches ahead of him, and finally pull himself up to the crutches and do it again until he made his way up those rocks."

I could tell by the way this hunter told me the story that his day was pretty much shot before it really got started. All he could do was shake his head and mutter, "the strangest thing I've ever seen."

Well, I of course knew it was my brother, Reed, but I certainly wasn't going to tell that old man that he was related to me. Reed must have covered darn near a half-mile up that ridge before he found a suitable lookout, or until he wore out the knees of his pants.

We talked a few minutes longer about the lunatics we occasionally encounter in the mountains, but I knew this old guy was sure he was never going to top this. I don't know if he ever got his elk or if he quit hunting shortly after that day. I do know that Neal, Matt and I helped our brother Reed up and down that mountain for a solid week, crutches and all. We created a trail that was so unique to that ridge line that from that season forward, it was nicknamed Reed's Rock. He didn't get a shot that season, but it wasn't for lack of trying.

Jack's Mountain

by Vivian Pfankuch
Sardinia, Ohio

I made my husband promise. The next full moon, he would take me camping up on Jack's mountain. It wasn't really a mountain, but we nicknamed it that when his dad bought the land in Scioto County. It was about 50 acres, almost straight up, with a meadow at the top. The meadow was loaded with deer sign and several strategically-placed deer stands. It was the place I shot my first buck.

We had to walk up the old logging road to reach the top. It took two trips to carry all the camping supplies and other necessities I (a city girl gone country) required. After several stops to catch our breath (and to look at the deer and turkey sign) we reached the top.

We reminisced about the day I shot the deer as we were setting up camp—a tent built for two, snacks, pre-fried frozen chicken. On that cold day in November, I had hiked up the hill with him and a huntin' buddy. It was cold, but I felt drenched with sweat from the climb. He asked, "Can you get in the tree by yourself?"

"Of course!" I replied. There was some silly male saying that had something to do with tall weeds and big boys that was an inferred challenge to me, and I was determined to do it alone. It was a struggle to climb to the stand, with a gun I had borrowed from his dad, but I did it. I got situated, tied myself to the tree, and was sitting with my back to the field. I wondered, "Can a deer see your breath when it's only 25 degrees?"

I was fascinated watching squirrels chasing each other around and around trees. People who had real jobs had no idea what they were missing! One squirrel climbed the tree I was in, and when he reached my foot, chattered and carried on as if to cuss me out! He soon got tired of me and ran away. About an hour later, after sitting motionless, the slightest noise made me slowly turn around. Walking toward me was a buck. He was sniffing the very trail I had walked down. Every time he put his head down, I turned a little more in the treestand. Jack had said, "Let him get as close as you can. Just keep letting him walk to you. Don't shoot until he looks you in the eyes!" Remembering these words, I waited, not moving, unless his head was down.

Time stood still. He would walk a few feet, I would turn a few inches. I was finally in position, my left arm braced against the tree, my right hand ready on the trigger. When the buck was about 20 yards from me, he suddenly raised his head and looked me straight in the eyes. It was now or never! I aimed, pulled the trigger and saw the buck jerk backward as the bullet hit him in the neck. He regained his balance and ran down the hill to a brush pile. The rest is history.

Now as I sat on Jack's Mountain, in the heat of summer, all those feelings came back to me. The mosquitoes buzzed against the screen of the tent and I remembered the feeling of not feeling anything or everything at once. I was not cold, hungry or tired then, and now I was not hot, hungry or tired. The adrenaline rush, the fear and the absolute ecstasy of being in the woods was overwhelming.

The sun had set and the moon was on the rise. I heard the sound of a lonely hoot owl and the coyote on the next hill. The whippoorwills seemed to be right behind our tent. We were bathed in a soft blue light from the full moon. Was that rustle I heard in the woods from a deer, or was it maybe just a possum or raccoon? I would not sleep that night. My pulse was just as fast as it had been the day I shot the deer. I felt as blessed and honored to be there that night as I had felt that morning. The greatest gift my husband could have given me was the opportunity to be there. I wanted to absorb all the sights and sounds of Jack's mountain again.

My First Mountain Lion

by Mary LaVerne McGuire
Kingman, Arizona

M y husband, Rudy, and I are avid muzzleloader hunters. One year, we put in for muzzleloader deer tags in Unit 44A, which extends from Highway 93 to the west and south of Alamo Lake. It is low desert country, and it is not noted for high deer success. Rudy and I did get tags and decided to pay $1.50 and take a mountain lion tag along, just in case. It turned out to be a smart decision.

I'd been hunting deer for about eight years. At that time, I'd taken three bucks. On the third day of the hunt, Rudy got a shot at a nice buck. We thought he had missed, so we went after the buck to make sure. At one point, Rudy and I split up. I started walking the side of the ridge, while Rudy walked on top. I spotted movement in the brush and watched as a lion sneaked out into the trail in front of me. I couldn't believe my eyes! I raised my .45 caliber rifle and fired. On the bullet's impact, the lion jumped and turned two or three somersaults off the trail into the brush, where I was unable to see it any more. I started to reload before taking a closer look, but couldn't because I had powder and caps, but had left my bullets in the Jeep. Being a little reluctant to look for a possibly wounded lion, I marked the place where I was standing with my hat, and went to look for Rudy and bullets. Upon reaching my husband, I excitedly tried to tell him of my fortune, but he didn't believe me. I convinced him to follow me back to where I had been. He thought I had just shot a large jack rabbit or a coyote.

I pointed in the area where I had left my hat, and we walked that way. Rudy was astounded. There, on the side of the mountain, was a full-grown female mountain lion, dead. My shot took the lion through the neck, producing an instant kill. She was about 100 pounds and over six feet long.

After tagging and field dressing it, we took it back to camp. The next morning, I took it into Kingman to our good friend, Jim Bevans, who skinned it out. Unfortunately, the skull was not measured, so we did not know if it would have qualified for the Arizona book of records. After reporting it to Arizona Game and Fish, I received two Arizona lion hunting patches. We had the skin tanned and made into a rug.

Now, back to the deer hunting. Rudy and I went back into the field and five days after the hunt had started, Rudy took a nice 3x3 buck. I was determined to take a big buck to end my hunting for the year. I passed up several small bucks before I spotted the one I wanted. On the last day of the hunt, I took a big 3x2 buck. Mine was larger than Rudy's in size. I would say it was a pretty exciting hunting season for me.

First Deer:
A Hunter's Story

by Andrew Jantz
Arlington, Massachusetts

My father and I are different in many ways. He was a sergeant in the Washington, D.C., police force for 28 years, I work for a publishing company. I read and write poetry (I have written two books), while my father, I would venture to say, hasn't read a poem—except mine, of course—since high school. We don't have much in common.

When I was a kid, he took me hunting with him sometimes, mostly for rabbit, once for deer. But hunting just didn't stick with me. It was his passion, not mine. After college, I moved to Boston, began a career and started a family. Then, one year in my mid-twenties, a friend got me interested in skeet shooting. I did this for a couple of years and soon felt an itch to go for something live. When another friend invited me to go deer hunting at his camp in the Catskill Mountains of New York, I jumped at the chance. I didn't get anything, or even see anything, but I was hooked.

A couple of years later, my father, knowing I was now hunting, invited me to go with him to one of the deer camps he frequents, run by a friend of his on a beautiful site on the banks of the Potomac in rural southern Maryland. I had a chance at my first deer, a running shot at a doe during a drive, and missed. Still, it was a wonderful trip, and I felt a bond with my father that was new to me—a common passion for deer hunting.

For several more years, I went with him to this camp as well as my friend's camp in New York, and though I had a couple of chances, I'd still not taken my first deer. After six years, I began to feel pressure. Not from my father or my friends, but from myself. I'd gotten over the initial thrill of just being present on a deer hunt and seeing deer, and felt that I wasn't a real hunter—a member of the club—because I hadn't had that first kill.

So the next year I went down to Maryland again, and on the plane down I remember praying that I'd get a deer. I wanted it so bad it was practically all I could think about. On the morning of the next-to-the last day, I had a shot at a doe—and missed. I was despondent. I was convinced I'd blown my chance, and would have to live another year thinking about my failure and waiting for another chance.

That evening, just before sundown—after a long, discouraging afternoon in my stand at the edge of a power line cut—I heard a rustling off to the left. Before I even looked, I was certain it was just another irritating false alarm caused by a squirrel. I was wrong. A beautiful eight-pointer had come into the open about 60 yards away. My heart nearly came out of my mouth. As I positioned myself to get off a shot, he crossed out of sight, and my heart sank. But then I saw he was making his way slowly along the edge of the cut, heading straight toward me. He suddenly turned back out into the open. I followed him in my scope, fighting to keep my excitement from affecting my aim. I held my breath, and squeezed the trigger. Through the noise and smoke, I saw him buckle right in his tracks, shot through the neck. I could hardly believe my eyes. I waited a few minutes, shaking with pride and excitement, then climbed down and walked into the clearing. As fate would have it, my father had not been far away, and when he heard the shot he came out into the cut and started walking my way. As soon as I saw him, I burst out, "Dad, I got him!"

He gave me a thumbs up sign as he walked, and I could see the pride in his smile. He took a picture of me with the deer, and then we gutted him together. I didn't care to stand and watch. This was MY deer.

When we got him back to camp, we hung him up in an open shed and then went into the cabin and toasted my success with 20-year-old bourbon. Dad called home to tell Mom, and I sat there, practically

142

bursting at the seams with pride. I couldn't believe it. My first kill a trophy eight-point buck. All the years of waiting made the moment that much sweeter, and to have killed him while hunting with my father just made the whole experience perfect. It was one of the greatest moments of my life, one I'll never, ever forget.

Back home in Boston, sitting down to a meal of venison and wine with my wife, venison I'd taken myself, all the pride came flooding back. And of course, being a poet, I had to write something. Here's what I wrote:

The Deer, By Candlelight

The circle is closed
in lifting the fork
and thinking back
to the distant
field where
you appeared in
antlered glory
as from a feudal
tapestry
and strode to your death
in the fading light
to sleep
in the crimson leaves.

As for the trophy, he hangs on my study wall, mounted on a beautiful board crafted by my father, complete with a little brass plaque. And I know that however many deer I may take in my life (and I've bagged a few more since then), there will never be another as special or as thrilling as the one I took that year, the one that made me a hunter.

Deerfoot Camp

by Barry Moyer
Emmaus, Pennsylvania

Buck season started with the "Deerfoot Camp" members arriving in camp in Tioga County, Pennsylvania, the day after Thanksgiving. The buck season was to open the following Monday. The camp members included myself, Barry Moyer, my wife, Jean, my two sons, Dave and Jeff, my brother, Arlin, his son, Chad, a 17½-year career Marine on leave from Virginia, and our good friend, Barry Schaedel.

Buck season opened with all hunters at their usual deer stands except me. I was restricted from walking in the woodlands due to bone cancer. I had to hunt off a chair on the front porch of the cabin.

Jeff, my older son, hunts with a .44 Mag. pistol. Monday morning, he missed a "Y" buck. Tuesday morning he missed the same buck again. Since we were in contact with two-way radios, I suggested he come back to camp and use my trusty .30-06. A while later, he arrived back at camp, and after hot soup and a sandwich, he headed up the trail again toward his stand with my .30-06. Halfway to his spot, he saw another buck. He fired the -06, and after calling on the radio for help in tracking the deer, his younger brother, Dave, and the rest of the party tracked and found the buck. A four-point, but not the same one he had missed earlier.

My nephew, Chad, harvested an eight-point on Thursday afternoon. This ended the buck season.

We prepared for the antlerless season to begin. Monday morning found me hunting off the front porch again. The first day ended with

144

no success. However, the second day had the hunting gods shining on the camp.

Dave took his deer at 7:45 a.m. We all heard the results on the two-way radio. Then, at 8:15 a.m., my wife announced that she had been successful with a huge doe. Dave and Jeff assisted her, gutting and dragging her deer to camp.

I decided I had to get up on the hill somehow to hunt. After lunch, Dave agreed to take me up on the three-wheeler. Jean and Jeff said no, it was too risky. Since we had recently logged, Jeff decided to try to drive up with his Explorer. In a short while he returned and said, "Let's go. Dave and I will drive you close to Mom's treestand. We'll help you up the ladder and into the stand."

The move was completed, and after 45 minutes to an hour, they had jumped eight or 10 deer. I was ready with my trusty .30-06 Remington. I waited anxiously, and finally spotted deer running in several different directions. One broke off and ran dead at me on one of the new logging roads. The -06 cracked, and the 1997 deer season ended with me calling on the radio, "Come on back, the hunt is over."

My two sons arrived with the biggest smiles. After taking pictures and field dressing the deer, we arrived back at camp.

What a way to end a hunt, with Dad being restricted in his 48th year of hunting. It is with great love and respect that I say, Thank you sons, from the bottom of my heart. Next year will be even better.

Lessons Learned

by Richard Perry
Fenton, Michigan

Being a father of two boys is definitely a blessing when it comes to having companions to hunt with for a lifetime. Having a wife that joined the hunting ranks four years ago was also a major blessing for me. I consider myself very lucky to have my family enjoying the great outdoors with me.

We get the opportunity to share our experiences and knowledge with the ones who are closest to us. I have taught them to shoot guns and bows safely since they were five years old, with the hopes that they will grow with respect for firearms and wildlife. They start by plinking with their little Chipmunk .22 caliber and move up from there. Teaching a youngster, boy or girl, gives you a deep-down feeling of happiness you can't explain. A lot like the feeling I get sitting in the woods with Mother Nature. Trying to explain our love for hunting is a very hard thing to do. I believe you either get the feelings or you don't. Those who have not tried hunting will never know the adrenaline rush from a whitetail standing seven yards away, or the woods coming alive with wildlife as daybreak hits. Peace and quiet, relaxation, being away from all the hustle and bustle of everyday life ... these are some of the things I hope the youth of today learn, and we all need to help. We can also learn from them.

My oldest son turned 12 last year. He took his Hunter's Safety class with his mom, who volunteered to take the class with him. I knew he wanted to hunt in a bad way. Hockey season is six months long and every

146

weekend, so I told him, "You don't have to play hockey," and before I got it all out of my mouth, he said, "I'm not playing." What a happy camper I was, after a pretty successful fall hunting season with my son.

We applied for Michigan's 1997 spring turkey hunt as partners. Luck was with us; the permits arrived in the mail. We applied for the last hunt for two reasons: 1) the hunt was longer and 2) hopefully the weather would be warm enough for the turkeys to start their mating.

May 8th, driving up north to our turkey camp, it was snowing hard. When we arrived at camp, the ground was snow-covered and it was pretty chilly out. Not what you'd call turkey hunting weather. The next day the snow turned to steady rains and it rained for the next two days.

Every morning we got up early and headed for the spot we had selected. The rain continued and the dampness just seemed to chill the bones after a few hours out in the woods. We faithfully got up, even though the conditions were dismal to say the least. A couple of things I did teach my family were that persistence pays off and that you have to have the right gear to be able to sit in any weather conditions and hunt successfully.

We saw turkeys every day we hunted, although they definitely were not interested in mating, due to the weather. We faithfully put our decoy out and called until around 11:00 a.m. Each day we saw turkeys in the distance, but the hens were all bunched up in groups and one or two toms were chasing the uninterested hens. The hens had a quickened pace to stay just ten or 20 yards in front of the toms.

The fourth day of the hunt would prove to be the day. As my son and I walked to our favorite spot, we came to the area that held the most tracks. I told my son, "We're sitting in that big pile of logs next to some two-track. No decoys, no calling, we are going to just sit and wait. The turkeys have walked the same area every day, so we will sit here until they pass by, and we'll see what happens." The two-track was only about four yards from the wood pile. I set my son up to my left, where the logs were low enough for him to shoot over, and in front of me was a pile of logs about three feet high. If the birds traveled the same way as their tracks indicated previously, it was a perfect setup. The higher logs would cover us until the birds passed us, and then my son would have a clean shot, if it presented itself.

147

Twenty minutes passed. I could see to my right, and just over the rise in the two-track came seven hens. I could hear them, "peck, peck, peck" as they approached us. I whispered to my son, "Here they come, get your gun up and be ready ... Oh, Ricky, they're all hens. Don't shoot." Seven hens walked within six yards of us and had no idea we were there. Wow! I slowly turned my head to my right again, the hens were fifteen yards past us now, and I wondered if one of those toms were with them. Over the rise came another turkey. "Ricky, it's a tom. Get your gun ready." I didn't even have my gun in my hands. I wanted so bad for my son to take this tom, a feat that I had not yet done myself.

The tom came walking right at us. At maybe 10 yards, he stopped and let out an earth-shattering "GOBBLE!" The tom was on the same path that the hens had taken, and was preoccupied with them. At about six yards, I decided to get my gun ready, just to back up my son. I wasn't worried about the tom seeing me move my gun into position; I didn't think he could see through three feet of logs. With our guns up, the tom walked right in front of us and stopped. Believe me, when I say six yards away, he might have been closer. My son was there, gun up, aimed at the turkey … six yards away and no shot. I waited for what seemed like forever. Still, he didn't shoot. I waited. And waited. Still no shot. The turkey put his head up and was starting to get nervous. He quickly walked about four yards away from us. I knew something was wrong with my son's shot, and it was now or never. BAM! My 10 gauge barked out as the tom nose-dived into the grass.

I looked over to my son and asked him, "Why didn't you shoot?" He said, "I didn't have a good shot, Dad. The logs were blocking all of the turkey except for about three inches of his head, and most of my shot would probably have hit the log and we wouldn't have gotten the turkey. Go get the bird, Dad!"

That answer was better than I would have expected from some of the adults I've hunted with. For a 13-year-old to use sportsmanship and intelligence in his decision, at a time when excitement can take over and cause even an experienced hunter to make an iffy shot, was very impressive.

My son brought tears to my eyes when he said, "I don't care who shot it, Dad, we still got the turkey." I was a very proud father, and I'm glad my family gets to enjoy the great outdoors! My youngest turns 12 this year and will be able to carry his own gun afield. How nice it is, all four of us bringing home the wild game. All I have to do is teach them to cook it.

Surely I hope to spend many years hunting, teaching and learning with my family. It seems like we're off to a great start!

149

A Silent Jig

by Linda Hall
Almond, North Carolina

I started hunting with my husband three years ago. It took some mighty tall talking to get me to start hunting, for I wasn't sure I could shoot anything. I even cry watching "Lassie" on TV. But he finally convinced me. I will only hunt for food, not just to kill animals, so when I started deer hunting, I inherited my husband's deer rifle. Of course, he had to buy himself a new rifle, but that's okay.

My first season hunting was on some private land we leased in Jasper County, Georgia. It was pasture land with woods. My husband sat me behind a large brush pile late in the afternoon and told me to watch the edge of the woods and pasture land. He went on to his tree-stand. Lo and behold, just before sunset, out wandered a small doe a good 100+ yards away. I picked up the rifle to shoot and I was shaking so much I had to lay it back down. This happened three times before I said, "Okay, you can do this now," and I held my breath, took aim and shot. She went right down. My husband couldn't believe I got it with my first shot.

The next season we joined a hunting club in Elbert County, Georgia, in which we still hunt. This is where I shot the eight-point buck I'm so proud of. It was November 2, 1997. The day was cold but clear. I was hunting in my treestand, across a ridge from a huge white oak with an abundant crop of acorns. The rut was on. It was still dark at about 5:30 a.m. when I got up in my stand. The first deer I heard was more than likely a doe being chased by a buck. All I could hear was running across and in front of me. It was still dark and I could not see. Slowly, the sun began to rise, and daylight began to appear. At about 7:30, I turned my head to the left, and there, 100 yards away, stood a deer looking straight at me. It was a buck, but I didn't know it at the time. All I could see was his face, and he looked to be a good-sized deer. I figured as soon as I raised my rifle up to find him in my scope, away he would run up the ridge and into the pines. But he didn't. He just stood there in the thick brush and trees. He was standing broadside, so I found his front shoulder in my scope and took aim just behind the front leg. All I had was about a six-inch diameter space to shoot in. All the rest was obscured by brush and trees, so I figured I had to take the shot. Then I fired. He whirled around and took off running back the way he had come, so I figured I had probably missed him and hit the tree. He ran out of sight. I sat in my stand for 15 or 20 minutes, waiting in case I had hit him after all. Just as I was getting down, I heard a rifle shot not far from me in the direction the deer had run, so I figured I probably chased him right on top of another hunter who had shot him. Darn!

Just to make sure, I walked over to the area where the deer had been. There was no sign of blood, so I tied an orange ribbon to mark the area. I started walking in the direction the deer had gone, looking closely for a blood trail, but there was none to be found. I tied two more orange ribbons as I proceeded. Figuring I'd never find him now, I was about to give up and go back to my stand when I looked to my left and there he lay. Still not knowing what I had accomplished, I figured I had shot a big doe. I wish someone had a camera to take a picture of my face when I saw that rack. My mouth flew open. I couldn't believe it. I was so excited, I wanted to yell and shout, but I knew there were other hunters in the woods, so I did a silent jig, and waited impatiently for my husband to get done hunting his area and meet me at my stand.

I stayed within vision of my trophy, waiting, waiting, plotting and planning all the while how I was going to surprise my husband. Finally, at long last, I saw my husband walking to my treestand. He said, "So you got one. I heard you fire a shot." I told him yes. He asked me where it was. I calmly said, "Over there." He then asked me if it was a buck or a doe. I told him he would have to look and see. The look on that man's face, I'll never forget. "Well, I guess you did shoot one; look at that!" He then picked me up and whirled me around in the air and shouted. He had also shot a deer that morning, a spike buck.

We loaded our deer in the back of the pickup and headed back to camp. Everyone was happy for me and congratulated me. The owner of the camp took pictures for his bulletin board. I'm one of only six women hunters at the camp. I have to say the men really treated us women very fair and respectfully. My poor husband took some ribbing from the other men hunters. We also took pictures and I have to fight to get them. My husband has showed them to everyone. My deer is now at the taxidermist and will be ready in May. They said he had a tall, sharp-tined, symmetrical rack. He still had shavings on his rack from rubbing. He will go on the wall across from my husband's big eight-point buck. What a memory. I relive that hunt over and over again and enjoy it each time.

Antelope Camp

by Thomas J. Carpenter
Plymouth, Minnesota

For some hunters, an antelope is a novelty. Head west once or twice in a hunting lifetime and tack on an antelope to whatever bigger, more glamorous game you have in mind. There's a head on the wall and a story to tell.

For others, an antelope is a commodity. Pronghorn season is a necessary inconvenience that gets in the way of other hunts, but it is a good way to put meat by.

But for some, antelope is *the* hunt of the season, and the antelope camp tradition is the highlight of the outdoor year.

***

You don't hear much about antelope camp in the popular sporting press. A tent in the sage and crawling through rocks and prickly pear after pronghorns doesn't seem to compete with wall tents and elk in the lodgepole, backpacking for mule deer at timberline, a deer shack in the woods or a warm motel bed followed by fields full of pheasants. But me, I'll take the prairie, windy solitude and pronghorns.

That's where antelope camp starts—way *out there* on some lonely stretch of dusty prairie road where my brother and I meet in the middle ground called Wyoming. From here, our pickups rattle and bounce through the late afternoon sun, in search of "the spot."

The advantages to making camp out on the prairie range from the functional (you're right there with the antelope and can be hunting as soon as you put on your pants in the morning) to the esthetic (a moonlit, midnight walk down a prairie two-track where the scent of sage rides the cool night air is probably as close as I'll ever get to paradise). But self-preservation prevails when choosing the spot where we raise our tent, and the name of the adversary here is wind.

It's impossible to avoid wind altogether, but we find ways to hide from it. Usually this means settling on the lee side of some prairie geography—often in a cut to the south or east of some rim. Here we enjoy some shelter from the west and northwest breezes while staying at some elevation in order to avoid pooling of the coldest air if the night breezes die.

Don't let anyone tell you different:
early hunting is prime hunting.

Here we pitch our tent and then back up one truck nearby, tailgate down, as a cooking area. A camp table, grill and coolers round out the scene.

***

Then, as the sun dips below the rim, we clear out an area and dig a fire pit. Sitting in lawn chairs, our boots to the fire and our backs to the endless night, we warm our feet until the prospect of down sleeping bags on good air mattresses gives us enough courage to kill the fire and brave the frosty trip to the tent.

Now that we have been blessed with an addition to antelope camp—my teenage nephew Chuck, namesake of his father—the tent is a bit more cozy. But I still take my spot next to the far end, zip down a corner flap to the stars and sage, and wait for the bag to warm and sleep to come.

***

No alarm clocks on the prairie. As the dawn sky brightens and works its way into the tent, sleep leaves the three of us one by one. When all the snoring has stopped or breathing patterns have shifted, someone works up the courage to say, "Let's go."

There's not much time between waking and hunting. The downright chilly temperatures contribute to that in two ways. First—dressing is a shivering scramble. Second—we learned long ago that breakfast on the go (a jug of orange juice, some fruit and a box of pastries en route to and between the most preferred antelope pastures) is better than standing around trying to cook and eat in the frigid dawn, getting cold and wasting valuable hunting time.

Don't let anyone tell you different: early hunting is prime hunting. The antelope are out. They're not as skittish when the sun is still below the horizon. You can use that low light to your stalking advantage—as another source of "cover," this one over your back, on the wide-open prairie. And without mirage from the day's heat, the black horns of dark-faced bucks are easier to judge.

***

And so begins the hunt.

We'll stalk a strategic spot as often as we will an actual pronghorn buck. Each method of stalking offers a special excitement, the bottom line being the stalk itself. Planning it carefully and then sneaking close through the available topographical and vegetative cover without spooking an animal that can spot the slightest bit of movement at a mile is the essence of pronghorn hunting.

***

When stalking a strategic spot, the sequence goes something like this.

By our third morning of hunting, we've pulled off a few good stalks but backed off each hillside and dusted ourselves off, deciding to continue the fun and look for a bigger buck. A scouting walk on the prairie three evenings ago and a spot-check two days ago revealed a good-sized herd of does without a buck residing in a secluded draw a mile from any two-track. As the sun rises over our right shoulders, we walk upright, then crouched at the waist and finally on our knees. As we near the final rise from where we can see into the basin, we crawl on our bellies.

We peek over. There they are. One, two, three ... twelve ... fifteen does. "There's a buck," big Chuck whispers, and then my eyes pass beyond the does to a buck standing on a knoll, surveying his newly-claimed harem. There is no need to study him further—his thick horns rise nicely and hook into a handsome heart shape. This is a nice, mature buck.

I settle into the shooting sticks and my shot whizzes over his back. The pronghorn ignores it in the howling wind, jogs down off the knoll and promptly breeds a doe. The does continue milling, and once they clear—after a five-minute wait—my second shot is on its way and finds its mark.

As we walk up to the buck, I think how hard it is for pronghorns not to be beautiful, even in death. Stretched out in the sage, with one hoof out to take his last step, the pronghorn looks every bit as graceful as I'm sure he was speeding across the prairie.

***

When stalking an actual antelope, the sequence goes something like this.

We're rounding a bend in the old two-track we're driving, heading for a new section of the prairie to explore. Our eyes glance up a draw as it begins to open into view, and we all see white pronghorn bellies and rumps at once. Truck in reverse, we back behind the hillside, plan our route for a minute, then start the long walk over the sage.

After a mile's hike, a mule deer doe and her twin fawns watching us the whole way, we kneel behind the especially dense knot of sage we had identified as our destination. There are well over a dozen antelope does 250 yards ahead, some bedded and some feeding, but there's no buck in sight. Three more does, only 50 yards ahead, block any further progress.

We get young Chuck set with shooting sticks, and I let out a big wheeze on my antelope call. A buck jumps up from his bed in a gully, looking for his challenger.

As we estimate the range, Chuck nestles in to the 6mm. At the shot, the buck takes off unscathed, steering his harem across the rolling prairie.

We follow the herd the rest of the morning, playing a lopsided game of hide-and-seek that the pronghorns have no trouble winning before our legs give out. We're tired but think—what a great stalk, what a fun morning wandering the prairie on our feet; we're playing the game fairly.

***

The successful stalks are, of course, the most exciting to tell about. But the truth is, most stalks don't even develop to the point where one of us can take a shot or whisper, "Let's go look for another one." Usually the pronghorns make the decision for us—winding us in a wild gust of prairie wind, noticing movement as a human head peeks over the crest of a ridge or spotting some aspect of our motley trio of hunters, rifles and daypacks traveling through the sage on feet, knees or bellies.

***

By early afternoon we're hungry and ready for a rest, so we head back to camp for the day's big meal. Cooking, eating and clean-up is easier in the light and warmth of day, versus doing it tired at night. Tacos, steaks over sage-sprinkled charcoal, hamburgers, fajitas, fresh vegetables, salad . . . we eat well. There's no reason not to when you can haul it to camp in your vehicle instead of on your back.

***

A siesta is not unheard of, from hunters and antelope alike, during this midday lull. In any event, eyes and legs just need a rest. Then, as the sun descends and the shadows lengthen, we head out hunting again. The antelope are usually more active now, and some evenings it seems like they literally emerge out of nowhere—bands and bucks you didn't know existed—to places that were so empty earlier in the day.

Being *out there* now—with night coming on and the wind lying low and the big quiet so loud in your ears until they get used to the idea— is the loneliest time of day on the prairie. Of all the wonders of pronghorn camp, the evenings are the memories I take with me back to my non-prairie existence in towns and northwoods.

These are the times we'll see the gray mulies—where were they all day?—so graceful in the sage, coyotes—like them or not—trotting across the flats, a meadowlark flushing from the grass, a sage hen running almost soundlessly ahead as you sneak up a draw.

***

My nephew shot his first pronghorn on such a Wyoming evening.

We came upon the buck—a nice one—closely trailing a single doe in the last rays of sunlight, peeking between a cloud bank and the Atlantic Rim. Chuck set up carefully and leaned into the shooting sticks. The buck began trotting off at Chuck's first shot, but the young hunter stayed calm as he worked the bolt. I called to the buck, he stopped to look back, then it was over as the bullet made its odd, hollow "whump" in the huge silence.

The pronghorn looked pumpkin-orange and snow-white as we slowly walked up to him in the final glints of the half-sun raking across the sage. Another big game hunter had been born.

***

It's dark by the time we pull into camp, the truck's headlights sweeping across a grassy hillside and finally stopping to rest on the lonely tent. We light the lantern, build a fire to ward off the cold, clean up the day's dust from faces, hands and equipment and finally relax by the fire with sandwiches and snacks.

Once our re-living of the day's hunt is over and the strategy for the next day is set and we've covered various topics of importance and unimportance—almost all related to hunting—we'll once again brave the trip to the tent one by one, the last hunter dousing the fire for good.

If it's been a day when I have chosen to shoot, and if I have been lucky, I'll smell a little like antelope—somewhat musky, a little sweet and a little salty, and quite a bit like sage—as I curl up in the sleeping bag again. One of my brethren might wisecrack in the dark, "Is there an antelope in the tent with us?" And I'll think, I'm too tired to answer that.

***

But not every antelope camp night is idyllic. I'm referring in particular to the year antelope camp moved to the Motel 6 in town.

Now, September weather in Wyoming can be as lovely as God ever created—frosty clear dawns, warm sunny days, cool but bearable nights. Or it can be downright unpredictable and miserable. This particular year chose to offer us a little bit of both.

158

The second sunny afternoon of hunting finds us high on a secluded ridge, carefully playing cat-and-mouse in its folds with a nice buck and his band of does. When a couple snowsqualls hit, we don't worry; the sun breaks out after each one. Then a band of snow hits that doesn't stop in the usual 15 minutes. By the time we find our way back to the truck, we are soaked, and a couple inches of the white stuff are on the ground.

We slip and slide the truck back to camp—now covered under three inches of slushy snow—and say to hell with it. We grab a cooler of food and a change of clothes, drive 30 miles to town and spend the evening in our long underwear in warm motel beds, laughing at bad movies on cable TV.

"We should be toughing it out, out there on the prairie."

I feel guilty for a little while (just a little while) thinking, "We should be toughing it out, *out there* on the prairie." But every time the wind roars louder, the guilt ebbs a bit more. Like that other antelope camp, this too is much different from everyday life!

When we bundle ourselves up to face 30 mile-per-hour wind gusts and 14°F cold the next morning, we further congratulate ourselves on our survival skills. We are alive, we feel good, we feel like hunting, and by mid-afternoon the temperature is in the 50s and the only snow left is in the shade on the north slopes and the prairie is habitable (for mere men) again.

***

Just as a little bit of snow can't end antelope camp, the shooting of an antelope does not signal its end, either.

One memento I treasure as much as the memories, prime prong-horn venison on the grill at home, horns on the wall or pictures in a photo album, is the product of our annual video hunt. These stalks are every bit as exciting as those with rifle in hand, and in many ways are even more challenging because our camera's zoom lens doesn't have near the range of a .30-06.

We'll spend a day doing this—exploring the prairie, maybe poking around an old coal mine or abandoned homestead, stalking antelope bands when the whim hits us and opportunity presents itself. It's just plain, no-worries fun, and we learn so much about pronghorn behavior: bucks sparring then chasing across the prairie in clouds of dust; does and fawns vocalizing to one another; a buck relentlessly bird-dogging a "hot" doe back and forth across a basin; a late fawn trying to sneak a quick suckle from her dam's udder; bucks issuing their snort-chuckle challenges to each other.

***

And after the antelope have been harvested but before the trip is over we'll go "herdin' antelope," as my nephew coined the activity several years ago. Sooner or later, in pronghorn country, a small herd will run parallel to your vehicle as you jostle along some secondary road or ranch road. We accept the challenge and punch our own accelerator, laughing and marveling at the fleet pronghorns stringing it out next to us.

Antelope just don't like to lose a race. So when the speedometer hits 35 miles-per-hour or so (as fast as we dare to go on a rutted back road or trail), the pronghorns pour it on and zip across the road in front of us, then run straight away from the vehicle, their white rumps waving good-bye.

By the time we look back a second or third time, the pronghorns are standing way out there in the sage, staring at our dust plume, probably wishing we'd come back and race once more so they could beat us again.

***

That's always my wish—to come back again—as we pull antelope camp and then drive out along the lonely, dusty roads once again in separate vehicles. Our good-byes are always short because we are men and because we didn't come to say good-bye to each other. We came to be together in antelope camp; those are the memories we take home.

The good-byes are short for another reason too: because we always hope this is not the last antelope camp. I love a good rifle, wide open spaces, the prairie and the antelope that live there. Carrying that rifle all day, walking the wide open prairie and seeing what's over every next hill, watching antelope live their lives for a few wonderful days ... this is the calendar spot that truly marks the end of each year and thus the beginning of another, for me.

And when times are tough—when winter has me down and cabin fever sets in, when pressures of long working hours, mortgage-paying, kid-raising and everything else that fills life today become almost too big to bear and sleep is hard in coming—my thoughts will drift to antelope camp. I'll see the open prairie, hear the wind in the sage, sling a rifle over my back and start walking.

Taking Shots at a Nickname

by Mark Kendrick
Brownsville, Tennessee

Occasionally there is an event in a person's life that forever haunts him. On such occasions, if an alert individual is present, a nickname will be bestowed upon the hapless victim of fate that sticks with them for life. Just such an incident occurred involving my brother, an incident he would gladly forget—if only his hunting associates would allow it.

The day began as most Sundays do during deer season—up early, in the stand before daylight, sit for several hours questioning one's sanity, go home for a bite to eat, and get ready for the afternoon hunt.

However, this day was somewhat different. My brother and I had decided that instead of going hunting that afternoon, we would work on a tower blind that was still under construction. Needless to say, we carried our rifles with us, just in case.

The platform already built, construction began on the corner posts and safety rails of the blind. I was in the blind measuring and nailing up the pieces that Mark was cutting down below. We worked through the afternoon, accomplishing most of what we set out to do for the day.

It was nearing dusk when we decided to knock off for the day. As I was handing the tools down to Mark, I saw some movement on the far side of the field. Raising my binoculars for a better look, I confirmed my suspicions. A young buck had walked right out into the field, even with all the noise we were making.

I whispered to Mark, "Get your rifle. There's a buck in the field right over there!"

Mark wasted no time getting to his shooting iron. Very deliberately, he moved into shooting position, resting his rifle in the cradle between the truck door and the cab. For what seemed like an eternity, I waited for the shot. I thought, "He's going to let that buck get away!" as I watched through my binoculars. KABOOM! The report of the rifle was deafening. I couldn't believe my eyes.

The buck just kept right on eating as if nothing had happened. KABOOM! The buck still didn't know we were in the world. KABOOM! He finally lifted his head to see what all the commotion was about. KABOOM! He took two or three steps and looked our way. I wondered, is this buck crazy or deaf? I kept watching in disbelief. KABOOM! Still, he just kept looking at us.

I could stand it no longer. "Mark," I said, "give me the rifle. Let me shoot him."

"Just one more time," my brother pleaded as he reloaded. "I'll hit him this time."

"Okay," I said. "One more time. But then I get to shoot."

KABOOM! finally, the buck decided enough was enough, as he wheeled and ran into the woods.

Mark stood beside the truck, staring across the field in disbelief. "Man, I can't believe I missed that deer."

"I can," I said. "I sat right here and watched you."

We finished loading the tools, my brother shaking his head the whole time, wondering how this could happen to him. As we pulled onto the field road and headed home, I looked over at him and said, "I never dreamed that buck would have stood there and let you fire six shots at him." Then it hit me. "That's your new nickname," I said. "Six Shot."

"Oh, no!" He moaned.

It stuck.

Never Hunt Alone

by Richard Lengel
Belle Vernon, Pennsylvania

I t all happened way back in 1974. It was the first day of doe season, and what a day it turned out to be!

My brother Bill, our friend Ray and I went hunting in Waterford, Pennsylvania. In 1974, does were plentiful. It wasn't hard to see 20 or 30 deer in a herd. So before we went into the woods, the three of us made a $25 bet that the first one back with a deer would win $50, but also the last one back had to buy dinner on the way home.

I knew these woods pretty well. During buck season I had seen doe come by my stand like clockwork at around 8:00 every morning.

At about 8:15, I heard a gunshot from where my brother's stand was. Just then I looked up the hill and a small herd was really moving. I pulled up and shot the one in the middle. I ran up there and there she was, lying dead. It was a small doe. I had no intention of gutting her at that point, my main concern was winning the bet, so I grabbed her and started running back to the truck. There was a path to my brother's truck, and as I was dragging my deer down the path, I looked up and saw Ray on a rock. I yelled at him and asked if he had seen Bill. He said he hadn't. I slowed down my pace, assuming I would be the first one back. I figured Bill was taking the time to gut his deer before returning. I was about 75 yards from the truck and saw the lights flashing on and off. It wasn't hard to figure out that Bill had heard me shoot, so he started to drag his deer through a shortcut and beat me by about ten minutes. I reached the truck and started laughing, and then made him gut my deer.

In the meantime, we were waiting for Ray to get his deer. About 11:00 a.m., fog started to move in and we couldn't understand what was taking Ray so long to get a doe. We looked up the hill and somebody was dragging a deer down the path. At first we thought it was Ray, but then realized it wasn't. We got out of the truck to help the guy drag his deer because we had a four-wheel-drive truck and his car was nowhere in sight. We met the hunter and he said he was really tired and asked if he could lie down for a while in the bed of our truck, which had a topper on the back. Just then it started raining, and finally we saw Ray dragging his deer, so we went to help him. As we were dragging Ray's deer, the hunter, who was resting in our truck, got out and was yelling for help.

We ran to him and asked what was wrong. He answered by saying, "I think I'm having a heart attack." Our first thoughts were to get him help, so we took off with my brother driving and the rest of us in the back. My brother was driving very fast, and with the rain and the fog, I was sure we were going to wreck. We yelled and pounded on the back window for him to slow down or we'd surely all be killed.

The hunter was turning blue and kept asking for more air. He wanted the windows open on the topper. We were about eight miles from the closest place to get help. There was no hospital in town, but there was a nursing home. We pulled up in front and I ran in for help. I explained to the nurse what had happened, and she said to pull around to the back of the building. I thought they were going to take him into the building, but instead she came out with an oxygen bottle and mask. She crawled in the back and started giving him oxygen. The hunter was gasping for air and couldn't breathe because the nurse was sitting on the oxygen hose and was crimping it. I was thinking that this poor man was doomed!

Finally, an ambulance arrived and he was taken to the nearest hospital. The police arrived and the rumors around town were that a hunter was shot. We finally straightened that story out and returned to pick up our deer and the other hunter's too. We took his deer to Ligonier's Game Commission, where they were nice enough to even butcher it for him and pick up his car.

Later we learned the hunter's name, that he was a state trooper from Philadelphia and that he hunted in this area because this was where his mother lived. He survived the ordeal and said he would not hunt alone after that.

Thanks to our buddy Ray for not getting his deer earlier in the day, we feel we probably saved a life!

Human Retriever

by *Joseph Newman*
Huger, South Carolina

As the alarm went off, I just knew it was going to be a great day for goose hunting. I shut the alarm off with one hand and shook my wife with the other.

"Dear, how about getting the coffee started? Russ will be here in a few minutes."

My wife's response as to what I could do with the coffee did not sound like a lot of fun. However, being a brave man, or a foolish one, I responded with, "How about making bacon and eggs for us?"

As I picked myself up off the bedroom floor, I surmised that my brother and I would be eating Slim Jims for breakfast.

It was one of those perfect upstate New York mornings—20°F and a very light freezing rain. My brother arrived right on time, and after a few cups of coffee and a couple of Slim Jims it was time to hunt.

The night before, I heard a large flock of Canadas landing on the large pond a short distance from my house. Russ and I have had a lot of luck at this pond, so the hunt would be the same as always.

We parked by the road and walked the tree line some three hundred yards to an opening about halfway up the pond. As we came out into the open, the geese started to take off. We both shot twice, and four geese dropped.

Russ sent Blue, his half-baked retriever, out to the downed birds. Blue brought back the two geese Russ had shot and one of mine. For some unknown reason, that darned dog took my second goose out to a small island in the middle of the pond and started mauling it. Russ called the dog off and back to shore.

By now it had warmed up to a balmy 25 degrees and had stopped raining. I knew that look I had gotten from my older brother, and knew what I had to do. I stripped down to my long johns and started wading out to the island. When I was about fifteen feet off shore, cussing like a drunken sailor about the cold and that dumb dog, my loving brother yelled, "Joe, there's a severe drop off in front of you. Just dive in and swim!"

Being the obedient little brother, I dove in and swam out to the island. I grabbed my second goose and started to swim back to shore. When I looked up, I saw my brother laughing so hard he was doubled over. I stopped swimming and tried to stand up. I should have known better. The water was not any deeper than my knees. As I walked back to shore, Russ, still busting a gut, wanted to know how cold the water was. Needless to say, my reply had nothing to do with the water temperature.

This was not the first time Russ had pulled something like this on me. Such is hunting with my older brother. Now, living a thousand miles apart, I sure do miss our uncommon hunts together.

The Ultimate

by A. Kathy Moss
Canyon City, Oregon

> *The challenge of an elk hunt is what gives a man drive,*
> *To become part of the wilderness, when all the senses come alive.*
> *To be part of the earth, wind and the trees that grow,*
> *To analyze what nature gives and survive by what you know.*
> *The ultimate happened to me, a moment in the wind,*
> *That fleeting moment when time stands still and forget what has been.*
>
> *The creek was down below me, I'm a few feet off the trail,*
> *My partner, who's a good friend, lets out an eerie wail.*
> *When the wind shifts in my direction, there is a distinct odor of musk.*
> *We know we are in elk country and it's minutes before dusk.*
>
> *He's in the trees across the creek, slightly to my right,*
> *I freeze the best I can, to keep from his keen sight.*
> *My heart starts pumping with the rush of adrenaline,*
> *Forgetting all the hunts before, living in the moment then.*
> *He is six feet from where I sit, my knees start to shake,*
> *Breathing deep and visualizing all that is at stake.*
>
> *He crosses the creek and raises his head to test the cooling air,*
> *He then stares right through me as if I wasn't even there.*
> *His ears twitch back and forth and there is moisture on his nose.*
> *His muscles are effortless strength as steady as he goes.*

He is two feet from me now, and I can see his wounds of spar.
He is a young bull and yet to learn how things really are.
Then just as silent as he came, he disappears out of sight,
I try to gather my wits, to think if what I saw was right.
I had let him pass by me and said a silent prayer,
I thanked God for this moment that I sat in awe to stare.
Of this sacred moment the image is etched in this life of mine,
That I can reminisce about, of another place and time.

With all my love, your wife.

Cassie

by Dennis Schult
Clarkston, Washington

She was just a pup when I got her, but I hoped that she would live up to the Labrador retriever breed's reputation as a water dog. I named her Cassandra—Cassie for short. Little did I know when I chose her name that it meant "helper of men." I trained her for waterfowl hunting myself, using various training books for guidance. For her first three years or so, we shared many hours afield. I would take her out five, six, seven days a week, regardless of rain, cold or sometimes even snow and ice. The time we spent together was far more than just training. We learned to trust each other and to anticipate each other's actions. We learned about each other's strengths and weaknesses and over time grew to become steadfast companions.

However, all good things must come to an end. She had been having trouble with her eyes for some time, due to an inherited disease that had rendered her blind and finally developed into glaucoma. She was clearly suffering discomfort at this point, and since she was over ten years old, I thought it was best to put her down. Her passing was particularly significant to me, because she had been such a big part of my life. Our relationship had spanned over a quarter of my lifetime. It lasted longer than my marriage and longer than most friendships. We had shared nine hunting seasons together.

Part of my difficulty with her death was that I had never had anyone or anything close to me die before. I thought I was prepared for it. Silly me. When the vet pulled the tourniquet off her leg and I saw the

171

light fade so quickly from those sightless eyes, that was when it really hit me. As a hunter, I have seen death close up many times before. But in those instances, I was able to see the bigger picture—The Circle of Life—the fact that in order for some things to live, others must die, and that death is not really an end but a new beginning. This time I had trouble recognizing that Circle of Life. In an effort to placate my spirit and lay hers to rest, I buried her collar, along with a goose feather, and nailed her dog tags to a nearby fence post.

In the days that followed, I began to see some purpose in her life. I started to recognize the things she had helped me to learn about life and about myself. I recalled the times when I thought she was off on a lark and completely useless, while my hunting partner and I searched in vain for a downed bird, and even though we thought we had marked the fall well, she would appear from somewhere far off with the bird in her mouth. So I realized that I should learn to trust my instincts the way she trusted hers, and I recognized that humans do not have a monopoly on knowledge. I thought about how I had taught her hand signals so that my eyes and her nose could work together. So I had learned about teamwork and cooperation. I thought about how she would never give up searching for a bird until either she found it or I called her off. So I had learned about the pure enthusiasm of doing the work you were born to do, and that I should follow my "calling." I remembered how I felt when I learned she was going blind, and that she would no longer be able to do what she loved most—retrieve birds. So as I took care of her in her declining years, I learned about compassion and loyalty. Finally, begrudgingly, through her, I learned about death.

I was glad that I had another Lab, Mocha, to help fill the space that had been left empty. It was an adjustment for her, too, because until then, she had lived her entire life with Cassie. So we helped each other. I must admit, I struggled with her at times. She was three years old, but she often acted as if she was still six months. Even so, it seemed she was a little more attentive, a bit more persistent and trusting her nose more. It may be far-fetched, but I'd like to think that a part of Cassie's spirit had come to rest in Mocha.

The Innocence of a Child

by Scott Johnson
Hubbardston, Massachusetts

I t was the first Saturday of shotgun season for deer in Massachusetts. A Saturday not typical of the many others that preceded because this was my oldest daughter's first time out hunting. Keri wasn't coming along to shoot, but instead to observe what this hunting sport was all about. I had my work cut out for me.

Keri was ten at the time, and the oldest of my three girls. I always made a point of including the girls in my hunting adventures, whether it be scouting, scanning the fields at dusk for wildlife or shooting arrows at targets for fun in the back yard.

She was curious about my addiction to the sport, so when she enthusiastically asked if she could accompany me on Saturday, how could I refuse?

The weather forecast for Saturday was sunny, windy and cold. The day began with the temperature in the single digits, with a slight breeze from the northwest. My plan was to be positioned in our stand one half hour before legal shooting time to let the woods quiet down after our intrusion. The crusty snow made a silent approach impossible. I had Keri dress in layers to protect her from the cold, but in doing so she looked like an overstuffed pumpkin. The stand I chose was about a fifteen minute walk from our house. It was close enough that if Keri got cold, we could be home in no time. When we finally made it to our stand location and got settled, we had thirty minutes before legal shooting time. I didn't plan on us working up a sweat walking to the stand site, but it was taking a toll on Keri. We were sitting up against a big hemlock tree, shoulder-to-shoulder, and were using the tree to shield us from the wind. I told her we had to try and sit for at least an hour because that was a prime time for deer movement. She said that she would try, but her feet were starting to get cold.

Just as the sunlight was piercing through the darkness, Keri started to get fidgety. The cold was penetrating through her snow boots. I gave her my grunt tube and told her to blow on it to try and call in a deer. My real intention was that it might take her mind off the cold. She smiled when I gave it to her, and blew on the grunt tube with the intention of a great flutist. What came out of the grunt tube was a noise that sent shivers up my spine. It was a call that was beyond words. It sounded like a cross between a fawn blat and an elk bugle. Definitely not the call of a deer.

I put my hand on Keri's shoulder and whispered, "Easy blows, you don't want to scare them."

She looked at me with a puzzled face and blurted, "But Dad, here they come!"

Sure enough, the loud noise of ice crunching underfoot was coming our way at a fast pace. Three deer were running toward us, and were going to provide us with a close encounter. As they closed the distance from us to thirty yards, Keri yelled, "Do you see them? They're right in front of us! Are you going to shoot them?"

At the sound of Keri's voice, the deer stopped dead in their tracks. A big doe with two yearlings looked directly at us, wondering why we were there. The woods became silent as a staring match ensued.

"Are you going to shoot one, Dad?" asked Keri, breaking the silence. "They're right there!"

That was all the deer needed to decide that we were a threat. Their tails went up and the deer almost stampeded over us as they ran for safety.

"Why didn't you shoot, Dad?" asked a bewildered Keri.

"Because I used my doe tag during archery season, and my second tag has to be used on a buck," I explained.

"Oh yeah, I remember now," she said, smiling. "That was so cool, Dad."

"Let's stay a little longer to see if the buck is around," I said. "Try blowing on the call again, but this time do it a little softer."

"But why Dad?" she asked with the innocence of a child. "They liked my call."

I couldn't argue with her, nor did I want to. This thrill was hers. She would remember this for as long as she lived, and probably embellish the story. As a parent, I couldn't ask for more.

"Okay, do it your way," I said, smiling.

Again, the fawn-blat-elk-bugle emanated from the grunt tube. She was smiling as the notes shrieked out. She blew on the grunt tube a few more times and then rested. No sooner had she stopped, when the tell-tale sound of a single deer approached our position from downwind. This deer was smart, because it used cover to its advantage. We were positioned on the edge of a swamp, overlooking a stand of hardwood trees. Laurel bushes were on our back side, and this was the direction the deer approached from. The deer, a big buck, stood about thirty-five yards from us in a laurel thicket. He was completely obstructed and sensed where we were hiding. He stood motionless for what seemed an eternity. Something had to break.

Then it happened. Keri blurted out, "Dad, it's a hunter! I can see his fluorescent coat!"

We stayed quiet for another ten minutes, but neither the big buck or the hunter ever made a sound. I could no longer see the deer in the laurel thicket. He must have sneaked off. They do that sometimes.

The cold was definitely penetrating through Keri's clothes. She was starting to shiver and we had to go, but before leaving, I had to show her where the big buck was. "Keri," I said, "let's go and see if the noise was made by a hunter or a deer."

"Okay, I'll show you where the guy is," she insisted. "I can still see him!"

But as we stood up, I could see what Keri was looking at. A fluorescent surveyor's tape was blowing in the wind. Keri saw it, too. She looked at me and said, "Show me where the big buck was."

We proceeded to walk over to the laurel thicket and found the answer to the question. There, in the ice-crusted snow, were the tracks of a large deer, the big buck. He had walked to the laurel bush and peered through the branches to find the location of the disturbance. Once he deciphered what it was, he back-tracked and walked in his own tracks, thus not making a sound. It was easy to read in the snow what he had done.

On our walk back to the house, Keri said, "Dad, I don't think I want to hunt. I don't think I could kill anything. But I still want to go with you. I can call them for you!"

I was at a loss for words. Her innocence and honesty were heartfelt. A successful deer story? You bet. Keri understands what it is that we hunters do in the woods. She may not be able to kill anything, but she will never stand in the way of someone who chooses to hunt. What more could I ask for?

The Big One

by Roy Bowers
Sugar Grove, West Virginia

Harlan and I arrived in Alaska, only to find that a hunter's worst nightmare had occurred. The airline had lost our guns and bags. We could manage without the clothes, but not without our guns. Harlan, who is a young 65, had packed some of his medication in his bags. The airline promised us our guns and baggage the following day. We always allow an extra day going in for those kinds of problems. Jack Goodwin, our outfitter, and my guide, Rick Hilgerson, met us at the airport. When we arrived at the motel, we met Chris, a lawyer from Connecticut. He had hunted with Jack and Dave Goodwin of Big Game Northwest Outfitters for the past ten days and had bagged an eight-foot grizzly. He offered Harlan and me his two guns. Every hunt we meet strangers that soon become friends. Chris is one of those people. Without his guns we would not have been able to continue our hunt.

The next morning, the airline had no idea where our guns and bags were. I called my wife and told her we were coming home. She said, "No way," and told us to go buy what we needed and go hunting. We had waited too long for a chance like this. She contacted Harlan's physician and he made a call to the Whitehorse Pharmacy. They filled Harlan's prescriptions, and we stopped by the sporting goods store and purchased a few necessities.

We flew to camp with a few clothes and borrowed guns. We landed on the banks of the Tatshenshini River. We were ten miles from the Alaska coast in the northwest part of British Columbia. I have been to British Columbia on several occasions, and I feel that it is by far one of the most beautiful and unspoiled places left to see. From our camp we could see the mountain goats and bighorn sheep. The mountains are so majestic and they look as if they are touching the sky. It is so quiet and peaceful.

Dave Goodwin was already in camp. We settled in quickly, and Rick felt we should go find some bears. We spotted several grizzlies but nothing caught our eye, so we headed back to camp. Around the fire that evening, we listened to Dave and Jack tell their big bear stories. Dave had guided and outfitted for over 50 years, so he has some great stories. While we were talking, Jack was glassing the mountains for bears. About 7:00 p.m., he spotted two bears and one appeared to be very large. Jack thought that one was a sow and the other a big boar. I asked Harlan if we were going to try to make the climb after the bears. His exact words were, "If I were 20 years younger I would have been gone already." We watched them until dark; I felt the excitement building already. The bears were on a mountain top a long way from camp. Dave said that if the bears were still there in the morning, we may have a chance of catching up with them. Trying to sleep was impossible; I could not stop thinking about that big boar.

The next morning, we were up at dawn. The sky was clear with a light wind blowing. It was cold as usual. We spotted the two bears still on the mountain top. Dave fixed us pancakes and eggs for breakfast, and everyone wished us luck as Rick and I packed our gear. We did not take a lot because we knew we had a long climb ahead of us. We walked three miles down the river and then started up the mountain. The mountain was so steep that you had to do a lot of crawling. About halfway up I stopped to rest. I thought I was in good shape, but my legs were numb and I felt like I could not go one more step. Across the river, on another mountain, we glassed several more grizzlies. Rick felt these were smaller than the one we were stalking. We continued our climb for the "Big One." We had to go all the way to the top of the mountain because of the way the wind was blowing. We did not want them to catch our scent, so we made sure we came on them from downwind. We selected a place with the best open area, then sat down and began the wait.

Rick decided to use his rabbit-in-distress call, and after several minutes a bear came up over the point. I looked at this bear with my scope and did not feel this was the bear we were looking for. She was a big, beautiful sow, she sniffed the air and then lumbered back over the point. Rick waited a few minutes and then whistled again. The sow came back, and this time she stood up and sniffed the air. After a while, she disappeared again. A few seconds later, another bear came into view. The bear came within 50 yards of us, and he was awesome! This was what we were looking for. I had never seen a bear so massive. His head was huge. Rick whispered for me to shoot, and I don't know which of us was more excited. I looked at the bear through my 4x12 Leopold scope and thought I had to get him on the ground quickly. I eased off the safety and squeezed the trigger of the Model 70, .338 Win. Mag. I shot him three times in the chest as he came toward us. He never stopped walking. After the third shot, I thought I had missed him. I kept thinking I had hit the scope on something coming up the mountain. I fired a fourth shot and he turned and walked back over the point. I knew the last shot had found its mark.

So many things went through my mind. Had I missed the opportunity of a lifetime? Had I wounded the big animal? Would I ever find him? Rick and I sat for 30 minutes and discussed all the possibilities. There was no noise, nothing but silence. It's an eerie feeling, wondering if you are going to become the hunted. We had not seen the sow, and we were hoping she did not have cubs. Bear mothers are extremely dangerous. They can be as bad as a wounded bear.

We finally decided to go for a closer look. We started over the mountain to look for some sign. About 30 feet down, we found a trail in the snow. The bear had gone into a ravine. We didn't like the idea of going in, but we had to find him. We found him about a half-mile away. We approached him cautiously. I could not believe what lay in front of me. He was a magnificent grizzly. As I looked at the size of his front feet and claws, I knew this big boar had not lost many battles. He had scars on his face, and some of his lip and teeth were missing. I could tell by looking at him that he was an old bear. The hump in his back looked like it was a foot tall, and his coat was dark and thick. He had a blonde stripe about a foot long on his neck. We found that all four shots had hit him.

I looked at my watch and it was 8:00 p.m. We had been stalking this bear for fifteen and a half hours! In all the excitement of that morning, I had forgotten my camera. We took several pictures with Rick's camera and then took care of the bear. Rick and I put the hide and skull in his backpack and headed toward camp. We estimated that the hide and skull weighed 200 pounds. As we walked down the mountain, we kept an eye out for the other bear but did not see her. We knew we could not get back to the main camp that night, so we found a good spot and settled in for the night. Rick and I had not packed sleeping bags, so we built a fire and settled under the bear hide for the night. It was cold and we had frost, but the old grizzly hide kept us warm. We slept several hours, and at daybreak headed back to main camp.

Dave, Jack and Harlan were waiting for us. They measured the skull, and we knew then we had a record book grizzly. We spent the rest of the day cleaning the hide and telling our big bear story. The next day, Harlan and Rick bagged an 8½-foot grizzly. It was a nice bear. Everything turned out great, we bagged two bears and the airline found our guns and bags in time for us to take them home.

When we checked my bear at Atlin, British Columbia, the skull measured 25⁵⁄₁₆ and the hide measured 9 feet, 6 inches. The game biologist estimated the boar to be 25 years old. I had had another outstanding hunt with the Goodwins. As for my guide, Rick, thanks again for another great hunt. I think it's going to be hard to top this one, but I'm sure I can talk Harlan into going on another hunt with me.

Opening Deer Hunting—November, Minnesota

by Dale Christopherson
Dayton, Minnesota

It was opening day of deer hunting north of Elk River, Minnesota, in the Sherburne Parks Reserve area. As the light began to creep over the horizon, my son and I traversed our way across a pine plantation toward my favorite hunting area. My small flashlight dimly lit our way.

Three times I would get turned around and go in circles before correcting our path. My son patiently followed, not uttering a word. I said, "I don't understand it. I've come this way for years. Why am I having such a time this year?"

Finally, as the light began to brighten the dark sky above, we arrived at the area where I wanted him to sit. But I could not find the tree due to the shortage of light.

At this moment, my son said, "I'm staying here until light, then I will find a spot." I assured him that we were on top of it, that I would move a short distance away and whistle to him when I found it at daylight. As distant shots rang out through the breaking dawn, I began my search for the elusive stand and found it almost immediately. A few minutes later, I saw my son working his way through the brush away from me, through the oak brush and cuttings. I whistled and he turned. I'm sure he thought I was crazy. I waved him over and as he heard me, I pointed to the tree.

"Now, watch and stay there," I said. "Don't move and you'll get your deer. Just stay there."

As he climbed the tree, I left to search out a new stand farther in. It was new territory for me. Far behind me, my son and three buddies occupied good stands that I had searched out in previous years.

I didn't want to go far, because my son, who is color blind, would need help in tracking a deer if he shot one. Around 10:30 a.m., I heard three shots. Two were a sure miss, but the third was a sure hit. I waited a few minutes to see if anything would come my way. Finally I began a slow walk toward my son's stand, to help him if need be. As luck would have it, I again went in a circle and found myself back at my new stand.

Well, I thought, this is an interesting day indeed, as I again traveled in the direction of my son's stand. I arrived to find him gone. I figured he must either be tracking the deer or gutting it, so I circled his stand until I picked up the blood trail of his deer. I followed it about 40 yards, where it stopped at a dark red spot, and then took off again. At this point, I knew that if my son had been following it he surely would have lost the trail, because only small specks of blood were visible on the dry leaves.

As I walked slowly in the direction of the trail, and three more times I found where the deer had stopped and left a large spot of bright red blood.

These woods were heavily hunted and though very thick, I have lost a few deer to other hunters who have stumbled onto my kill before I got to it. I hoped as I tracked it that this would not happen to my son's deer. I had spent well over an hour slowly walking and searching for the trail when two hunters passed and asked what I was doing. I said I was following the deer my son had shot.

They smiled and headed off in the opposite direction. Fifteen minutes later, a hunter and his eleven-year-old son came toward me. I told them the same thing, and admitted that at that point, I needed to circle again to look for more signs ahead. As I began to circle, the hunter and his son took the time to circle the other way, and in a few minutes he hollered that he had found the blood trail.

I walked over to it. It was only a few drops, but there it was. I picked up my mittens and hat, and put a mitten down at the new spot. I began to follow the blood trail again. Again it ended, and the other hunter helped me find it again. As we walked, I said, "He can't have much blood left." I had no sooner said it than he said, "Guess not, for here he lies." He was a magnificent ten-point buck, weighing close to 200 pounds. I cannot tell you how happy we all were to find it.

The hunter and his son said good-bye. I thanked them for their help. I dressed out the deer and as I tried to drag it out, I could not even begin to pull the monster by myself. I sat down and saw my son crossing the pine trees. I hollered, and he came toward me. As he neared me, he told me of the huge deer he had shot, and that he needed me to help him track it.

I said to him, "Well now, we need to drag this monster out first." As he neared close enough to see the buck lying near me, he said, "It's a huge one, Dad. Mine was that big, too. Where did you get this one?"

I said, "Well, I heard you shoot and I tracked this buck all the way from your deerstand."

As I stood there with a grin on my face, my son came toward me, put his arms around me and picked me up and turned me in a complete circle with a big hug. He said, "Isn't it beautiful? Thanks, Dad! I thought I had lost it for sure!"

It took about three-and-a-half hours to drag that monster to the truck. We will hunt together again next year.

The First Deer Hunt

by Dave Keller
Bend, Oregon

> *Five a.m. comes early*
> *to a boy of just barely ten.*
> *But a lifetime love of hunting*
> *was ready to begin.*
>
> *I ate a "deer camp" breakfast,*
> *that's a donut and some juice.*
> *Then I put on my hat and my blaze orange vest*
> *and my brand-new "hunt'n boots."*
>
> *I climbed in the back of a pickup truck*
> *with my dad and all the rest,*
> *took a long cold ride down an old dirt road*
> *to where the "big ones" lived ... I guessed.*
>
> *As we rolled to a stop, we both climbed out*
> *at some predetermined site,*
> *where Dad and I slipped into the woods*
> *just minutes before first light.*

I remember the ground being cold that morning,
and having trouble just sitting still
when out of the morning hazy-gray light
stood a buck on the side of the hill ...

Some 25 seasons have come and gone
since that first one with my dad,
but I'll never forget all the lessons he taught me
and I miss all the good times we had.

So now, every fall, as the leaves start to turn
and summer quietly comes to an end,
the sounds of Canada geese headed south
means the season is about to begin!

With camp finally set up and a campfire built
hot coffee from a cup made of tin,
and one cup filled with hot chocolate
for my boy, who's just barely ten ...

A True Sportsman

by Chris Sutter
Greenwood, California

Growing up, I loved camping, fishing, hunting, guns and anything that would put me in touch with the woods. Because my father worked seven days a week for most of my childhood, I relied on my two uncles to take me on outings. They played a big part in teaching me, along with my younger brothers.

One uncle, Denzil, was a master sergeant in the National Guard. He impressed upon me the importance of the skill needed when using weapons, and that safety was number-one whenever handling a gun.

Once, when we were hunting together in the forty acres behind my grandpa's house, a rabbit jumped from the brush and ran. Excitedly, I shot at the rabbit for no reason other than just to shoot it. I hit it and was proud of what I had done. My uncle congratulated me, saying what a good shot it was. I smiled, thinking he was sincere. He didn't return my smile, so I asked him what was wrong. He told me that killing "just because" was not acceptable. He simply said, "We don't waste any animal we kill. Go and get it and we'll cook it up for the dogs." I had to dress and skin that jackrabbit, and if you have ever done it, you know it is not a treat. To this day, I do not shoot anything I am not going to eat.

My other uncle, Dick, the younger of the two, was always on the wild side. Mischievous as he was, he sometimes got into his share of trouble—but good trouble at times, too. I spent a lot of time with him and always felt a closer bond with him. Most of my outdoor trips with him had to be earned. He would take me to his house to do what I believed were "his chores." I would mow, rake, pull weeds, build walls, sidewalks—whatever needed to be done at the time. He loved building things with river rock; maybe he should have been a mason. After the chores were completed, we would load up in his old Jeep and head out. We might go fishing for shad in the river, in the woods to go stream fishing or just hang out at a sporting goods store and check out all the stuff. He always knew the latest fishing rig or the best new gun caliber. It was fun being in the store with him.

One evening, long after I was married, his wife called and told me that Dick had saved the life of a four-point buck that had fallen into the canal owned by the electric company he worked for. It was in the middle of winter and the water was so cold it could freeze a person's blood in no time. Ice would build up in the canal and have to be cleared away from the gates. Sometimes this would have to be done two or three times a night.

As he approached one particular gate, he spotted the buck because its antlers were sticking out above the canal edge. The deer was barely alive when Dick found him. He struggled with the deer, managing to pull it out with a rope onto the bank of the canal. The deer had ice caked on his chest and his eyes were glassy, but he was still breathing. Immediately, he started rubbing the deer down with dry snow. He then built a fire on the bank next to the deer and covered the deer with a blanket. For the next few hours, he would slap the deer, trying to keep it aroused. He would move the deer's legs and neck to try to keep the blood circulating. Soon the deer was on its feet, but still not ready to leave. Dick went into his house for the night and when he got up in the morning to check on the deer, it was gone.

I often wonder if anyone else in those circumstances would have done the same thing. It was a great opportunity for another rack to add to his collection and to fill his freezer with meat.

It is a true sportsman when a man can be a hunter of game, but also feel the need to save the life of a struggling animal. Even though he has shot many game animals over the years, he took this opportunity to release this animal back to the woods.

I am very proud of my family background and the values they have instilled in me. Sportsmen who think not only of themselves, but of the animals they hunt, are the true heroes. I hope to have the opportunity to pass on all I have learned to the younger generations of our family.

One Last Time

by Kal Sears
North Platte, Nebraska

A s darkness approached, I slowly gathered my equipment and put
the cameras away like I have done a thousand times before. Only
this time, it was different. What had started 12 years ago with a smile and
a handshake had ended with a phone call. We had lost our favorite
whitetail hunting area. My brother Don and I had gone to the neat farm-
house to ask permission, which we not only got, but found a friend as
well. We took an instant liking to John and remained good friends for all
the years. Two years ago, right before Christmas, we lost John to cancer,
and from then on, things changed.

Now it was New Year's Eve and the last day of deer season. Don
and I had chosen to spend it at John's. An almost eerie calm settled on
our stretch of the Platte River. A lone goose called to its lost mate,
which I knew it would never find. A squirrel, chickadees and a cottontail rabbit stopped by to say good-bye, and outside of a doe and her
twin yearlings that walked under my stand, no other deer were spotted.
For this I was thankful, as it wouldn't seem right to take a buck under
these somber conditions.

This area really wasn't that good for archery deer as they mostly
fed and bedded down on the south side of the river. But the chance of
a good buck or a fall turkey was there. It was such a pretty place, and
almost like a park, which Don and I helped by picking up any litter
that we found. We had six stands and each had a name, such as

"Turkey Roost," "Bobcat," "Leaning Tree" and "The Hilton." We would leave all of them in place tonight and return next week to remove them and clean up.

No money was ever exchanged with John. Instead, we provided a turkey every Thanksgiving, a big box of fruit at Christmas and a favor whenever possible. We put cattle back in, repaired a fence, and brought John small gifts at different times.

The phone call we received was from the manager who had taken over the day-to-day operations of the farm. He was polite but said that a large company from Louisiana had approached him wanting to lease the property for deer hunting. The price he quoted was so far-fetched that he had no choice. I knew that in this day and age, when it seems that everything is governed by the almighty dollar, the time would come when we would no longer hunt John's place. I have no answers to this leasing thing that has taken over hunting all over the country. Nor do I have a solution as to what the average bowhunter can do in places where very little state or public land is available. But what I do know after 40 years of bowhunting is that it is a sad situation. We have lost five places ourselves and I know of others that the same thing has happened to.

The sun was down and as I slowly walked to meet Don at the truck, I said a silent "thanks" for 12 years of enjoyment. Thanks to all the Johns and the great people like him in the world. I'm glad I was a part of it and am able to see more good than bad in this world we live in.

No Place for Pessimism

by Jeff Anderson
Rigby, Idaho

I've never considered myself a very lucky person. This is usually proven each July when the results of Idaho's controlled hunt tag drawings are announced. However, I am extremely lucky in that my wife, Rachel, enjoys the outdoors and has been my companion on several hunting trips in our young marriage. After many years of rifle hunting, first with her father and now with me, Rachel decided she wanted to try bowhunting, not as my unarmed companion as in past years, but now carrying a bow. After taking Idaho's required bowhunter safety course, purchasing a bow and many nights at our local archery range, I could see her enthusiasm growing as we both eagerly anticipated the August 30 archery opener. She quickly became proficient at the range out to about 25 yards.

When the opener finally arrived, I headed up the divide about 150 miles northwest of our home for a six-day backpack hunt with some friends. Rachel was very supportive and put on a good show, but I knew very well she would have gladly taken my place and left me home to work and watch our two young children.

On the trip up, I truly regretted leaving her behind. How many guys are lucky enough to have a wife who wants to bowhunt? I had done everything I could do to encourage her interest in this sport I enjoy so much, until now. I felt I had abandoned her and wondered if I might have stifled her enthusiasm.

The trip went well—beautiful country, lots of bulls, but none were ever close enough to be in any danger from my bow. After six days at five to ten miles per day of walking, I was beat. When I arrived home, all I wanted to do was put up my feet and relax. Rachel had other plans. After working all week and spending her evenings chasing our two kids, she did not want to wait another day. I was informed that a baby-sitter had been arranged and we were heading out at 5:30 a.m. to hunt an area about 20 miles away from our house. Remembering how I had felt the week before, I quickly agreed and fell asleep.

The alarm rang and it was all I could do to get out of bed. We loaded the truck in the rain and headed out into a foggy, wet morning. The area we would be hunting was good elk country, adjacent to agricultural lands; however, the easy access and proximity to large (for Idaho) cities caused it to be hit hard during the general rifle season. We found our turn-off, rolled past a small ski resort and splashed along a muddy gravel road until we reached an area near where we had seen elk during last

year's rifle season. It was raining lightly as we headed up a wet trail and were instantly soaked from the waist down due to the dripping underbrush. My tired legs were already screaming as I tried to keep up with Rachel. After the initial incline, we reached a small plateau and made a plan. Rachel would still-hunt through a known bedding area, and I would circle uphill and watch a game trail we had seen elk use as an escape route in the past. As soon as we split up, I thought I heard animals moving about in the timber, but I had seen no tracks or sign in the hour since we had left the truck. Using cow calls to monitor each other's whereabouts, I heard Rachel nearing the edge of the timber and went down to meet her. "There are fresh beds and animals crashing all around in there!" she exclaimed with obvious excitement. I told her I hadn't seen a thing and we had probably scared everything out of the country. I expressed that since we were both wet, tired (I was and I assumed she was, since she was four months pregnant), and it was now raining hard, we should head for the truck and get some lunch. Rachel gave me a dirty look as I continued my case saying, "It is still too warm, the elk must be up higher."

Rachel turned and started off down a trail and I followed. As we probed deeper into the dark timber, we began to hear some consistent twig-snapping above us on the ridge. Without words, we made a plan and Rachel headed slowly straight uphill toward the sounds and I circled downhill. Rachel had barely disappeared into the tangle of pines when loud crashing noises began, followed by several cows (of the slow elk variety) showing their white faces and plunging downhill past me. I caught up with Rachel and said, "Those cows made enough noise to scare off any animals for miles, and I'm drenched. Let's go." Rachel responded, "Let's at least check the creek for sign," as she pressed on down the hill. The creek was ¾ of a mile away, and we continued to push cattle toward it regardless of how carefully we chose our path. I was now just along for the ride. I had given up on cow calling, listening and even believing there was a remote chance we might see elk. Rachel continued to cow call and received bellows from bovine as they dropped Frisbee-sized "sign" and crashed on ahead of us.

We reached the creek and were unable to find any elk sign. I was actually relieved and ready to find a short cut to the truck. Obviously disappointed, and with my pessimism wearing on her, Rachel finally seemed resigned to my wishes. Then it happened. A long, drawn out bugle pierced the wet air and I could see Rachel's eternal optimism return and instantly grow exponentially.

"Don't just sit there, bugle back!" she whispered. I obliged, after telling her I was sure it was just another hunter. A half-hour of bugles and cow calls went by without an answer. Wet, muddy, hungry and tired, I again tried to convince Rachel that we should head for the truck. She reluctantly agreed, but, not willing to give up completely, we took a different path back that put us side-hilling midway up along the ridge the bugle had come from. She continued to cow call and persuaded me to bugle occasionally. Beef cows continued to materialize and rumble away ahead of us. After stopping for Rachel to try some cow calls, we heard a noise easily definable as an animal about 100 yards off in the timber. "That sounds like antlers pushing through branches," Rachel whispered and made a 90-degree turn to head toward the sound. I responded that it was quite obvious there were no elk around here and we would be wasting our time chasing cows through the brush. Undaunted, Rachel kept moving and I followed like a lost puppy. After 50 yards, Rachel asked me to try a bugle. As I rolled my eyes and set down my bow, I noticed she had held up her hand and frozen. I looked up to see what was going on, and there, 30 yards away, standing in the middle of the trail, was a magnificent six-point bull, staring right through us. Time stood still and as I slowly crouched to pick up my bow, he bolted. Several cows (elk this time) and a rag horn materialized and immediately hit top speed. We watched in awe as they crossed an open hillside and within minutes put over a mile between us and them.

It was obvious that this bull had come silently to our calls and had completely disregarded the cattle. After examining the fresh tracks, drinking in the strong, musky odor and marking the escape route they had taken on the topo map, I realized that today I had been the type of hunting partner that I had complained about in the past. I had in fact been more of a hindrance than a help in my wife's quest to harvest an elk with a bow. I apologized to Rachel and admitted my mistakes right there on the trail. Rachel, fortunately, does not measure success by meat in the freezer but by time spent in the outdoors and the opportunity to observe these wonderful animals up close. I was quickly forgiven. I made some silent promises during the trip off the hill that day and realized just how lucky I was to have my best friend, wife and hunting partner all in one beautiful package.

One of the Happiest Days of My Life

by Matt Hemmer
St. Charles, Missouri

It all started the first weekend of deer season. My dad told me the night before that we were not going to get to go deer hunting that weekend. He said we would go the next weekend for sure.

I came home from school and saw that my dad was getting ready to leave. As always, I was dilly-dallying around. My dad started yelling at me. I kept telling him, "I'm coming, just hang on." We finally got the truck loaded up with all of our gear. We left about 4:00 in the afternoon. On our way up to our farm, he had the radio blasting. Then, all of a sudden, he turned the radio down and started talking to me.

Every year, my dad gives me a lecture on what to do if I shoot a deer, and on the safety procedures. Dad and I go up to my grandma and grandpa's farm to go hunting. It took us about 15 minutes to put all our clothes on and put our bows together. By the time we got done putting everything together and our clothes on, it was about 5:30. Dad told me to go to "The Door," which is my favorite treestand. Dad said he was going to go to the blind in the corner of the field. I went to The Door and got all set up.

All of a sudden, a squirrel came out of a tree and sat right in front of me. It stared at me for a long time. Then, the next thing I knew, the squirrel was wanting to get on top of me. So I made a little sound and the squirrel ran down the tree and started barking at me. I started to stand up to scare the squirrel, and then I heard a stick crack. I looked over my shoulder, and there was the biggest buck I had ever seen before. I slowly sat down. The deer kept getting closer and closer. Every time I looked at it, I started to shake a little more. I stood up to shoot it. The deer came within 15 yards and kept walking. I put my 15-yard pin on it and I was leading the deer a little bit. All of a sudden, I released the arrow and the deer snorted and sniffed my arrow, which was stuck in the ground. Then it ran off as fast as a cheetah.

The deer was the biggest buck I had seen in my life! I waited a little while and then got out of my treestand to get my arrow and to tell my dad what happened. When we finished hunting, we took all our gear off and put our bows away.

Afterward, on the way to my grandma's and grandpa's trailer, my dad was saying how happy he would have been if I would have gotten that deer. When we got to the trailer and were eating dinner, my dad told my grandparents about the deer I missed.

My dad and I got back to the cabin to unload all our gear and go to sleep. We got our sleeping bags down and checked them for wasps, hornets and rodents. There weren't any rodents in our sleeping bags, so we settled down and went to sleep.

My dad woke me up at 5:30 the next morning to get ready to go hunting. I ate breakfast and put a ton of clothes on. My dad told me what to do if I shot a deer. I told him, "I know," and went down to "The Cedar Tree" and got all set up.

I was waiting for it to be light out so I could shoot a deer if one came in range. I kept hearing a noise that sounded like a deer walking toward me. The sun finally came out, and I saw a six-point buck coming toward me. I about jumped up like a jackrabbit seeing a predator coming. The six-pointer was about 30 yards away. The farthest I can shoot a deer is 20 yards.

The six-pointer passed me and I heard another deer coming. It was a two-point buck. I stood up to get ready to shoot the deer, but I was shaking bad. The deer was about 15 yards away. I drew my bow back and held it for about six seconds, waiting for the deer to come out from behind a tree. I put my 15-yard pin on the deer and released the arrow. I heard a noise that sounded like I had hit the deer. I shot another arrow, which went into the ground, and then watched the deer run off until it was out of sight.

I waited for about two minutes, and then got out of my treestand to tell my dad. It took me about 15 minutes to get to his treestand. When I got there, he said I had just scared off a deer he was going to shoot.

I told my dad I had shot a deer. He said, "We should wait a little longer before we go find it, but I guess we can go see if you got this one."

My dad and I went over to where I had shot the second arrow. There was a ton of blood. We followed the blood trail about 30 yards and my dad said, "There's your deer." Then he said, "Congratulations."

We went and checked the deer in, and after that we hung it in a tree. A couple of days later, we went home. I had a big smile on my face. My mom thought I didn't get a deer, but I said, "Go look in the back of the truck." She looked, and she was so happy. My mom called all of my relatives. She was really proud of me. That weekend was one of the happiest times of my life.

A Trophy Moose

by Wayne Moen
Corvallis, Montana

Far in the distance, a speeding pickup trailing a cloud of dust revealed the location of my two hunting buddies as they rapidly departed the area.

Early that morning, the three of us had driven to the Big Hole Valley of western Montana to hunt elk and moose. Rancher Bud Moberg, who was born in the valley and still lives there, had given us permission to hunt on his 10,000-acre cattle ranch. Arriving at his ranch at sunrise, I visited with Bud in his cabin while my buddies waited in their pickup. Bud suggested we try the Flag Creek drainage, as he had seen elk and moose the past several days while searching for stray cattle. Bud said, "As long as you are up there, would you do me a favor and shoot the old crippled bull because I doubt that he will make it back to the ranch. Later on this afternoon I will be up to get him, before a coyote or wolf finds him."

I informed my friends that hunting looked good as Bud had seen game in the area. I had a moose permit, and my friends had their elk tags, so our expectations were high. From Bud's cabin, the sage-covered bottomland gave way to pine-covered foothills of the continental divide. Arriving at Flag Creek, we decided that I would hunt the willow stands along the creek, while my friends would concentrate on the high meadows along the divide where elk were known to feed.

After an hour or so hunting the willows, I heard several shots coming from a distant hillside. Maybe they got an elk, I thought, but I had yet to see a moose though moose sign was all around me. As I paused to catch a breath, I heard the sounds of an animal coming toward me. Whatever it was, it would walk awhile and then pause. Soon, the walking came to an end. Maybe a moose had bedded down. Cautiously, I made my way through the thick willows, rifle ready toward where I had heard the sound. There, within twenty feet of me, lay Bud's old bull, perhaps too exhausted to continue on. He spotted me about the same time I spotted him, and he made no attempt to move.

I settled down on a stump to see what the old boy would to. With an anguished look, he lay there staring at me but made no attempt to get up. I wondered what he might be thinking about, and perhaps he was wondering what I was thinking about. Maybe he thought I was there to take him back to the ranch, which for years he had managed to make it back to on his own. Or maybe he was wishing I would put him out of his misery. Staring at the old bull, I realized that Bud had asked me to shoot the bull because he had become attached to it over many years and couldn't kill it. I had known it for less than an hour and had developed a short-lived friendship. Hard as it was for me, a promise is a promise. I raised my .30-06 Remington and put the old boy to sleep.

As I worked my way back to the road, I was surprised to find that I had shot the bull less than a hundred feet from the road. At my truck, I sipped hot coffee and somehow lost interest in moose hunting for the day. In late afternoon, my friends returned, having killed two nice five-point bull elk. After listening to tall tales of their hunts, they asked me if I had shot a moose as they had heard my single shot that afternoon. I informed them that I had killed a bull weighing around a thousand pounds with a beautiful set of horns less than a hundred feet from the road.

They couldn't wait to see my trophy bull. Arriving at the site of my kill, they stared in disbelief that I had shot the rancher's prize bull. They wanted to leave the area before Bud showed up, but I talked them into helping me get the old bull out to the road. The truck's winches soon had the bull at the edge of the road, and I proceeded to gut it out. As I worked, my friends kept staring down the road toward Bud's cabin. About that time, far in the distance, they spotted a cloud of dust coming toward us. Little did they know that it was only Bud coming to pick up his old bull!

Upon realizing that the truck belonged to the rancher, my buddies got in their truck and at top speed departed the scene. Arriving at my truck, Bud inquired why my friends were in such a hurry to leave. I informed him that I had told them that the old bull sure looked like a moose to me when I encountered him in the thick willows. As we sat there laughing and drinking the last of my coffee, a cloud of dust could still be seen trailing my friends' pickup as they departed from Bud's ranch.

With the help of a winch on Bud's truck, we soon had the bull on his truck and were back at his cabin. In appreciation for killing the bull, Bud gave me several packages of frozen moose meat from a cow moose he had shot earlier in the season. One way or another, I had gotten some moose meat.

Two weeks later, near the area where I had killed the bull, I managed to shoot a moose. The following spring, while visiting with Bud, he told me he had a present for me. During the winter months, he had mounted the skull and horns of the old bull on a weathered pine board. Below the skull, and burned into the wood, appeared "Trophy Moose, Shot By Wayne Moen, 1957."

The Blue-Eyed, Bushy-Bearded Guardian Angel

by Rev. Walter Amidon
Travelers Rest, South Carolina

The rain came down in buckets on October 3, 1991, the third day of primitive weapons season here in South Carolina. Most of the fellows in our hunt club had decided to go home and sit it out by the fireside on this wet and blustery day. A few of us elected to stay and brave the elements, hoping the deer would still be moving. I had a good reason for staying. The night before I had missed a huge ten-point that had come from nowhere at dusk and stood directly beneath my stand.

Before Mike and I set out that day, we put pins in the club property board so that everyone would know where we were in case of an emergency. For safety reasons, we also had a club rule that someone would stay in or around camp until the last hunters came out of the woods and pulled their pins from the map.

The rain came down in sheets as the day dragged on, and the darkness soon started to creep up on us. I looked at my watch at 6:12 p.m., 24 hours since I had last seen the two bucks beneath my stand. Where were they tonight? Had I scared them off for good? When we had about ten more minutes of shooting light left, I looked over at Mike in a treestand about 20 yards from me with his bow. He looked like a drowned possum.

I was just about to give up for the day when something caught my eye. There stood a ten-point buck, twenty yards away, and I had a broadside shot. My hands trembled as I pulled the hammer back, hoping the buck wouldn't hear the lock click when I pulled it into firing position. Mike looked over at me as I raised my rifle to fire. I put the sights on the buck's front shoulder and pulled the trigger. The muzzleloader roared to life, and a line of fire and smoke spewed from the barrel. I peered through the smoke and saw the buck take off. My hands shook as I thought to myself, "Did I hit him?"

Mike and I climbed down from our stands. Mike took off in the direction the buck had run, and I walked over to where the buck had been standing. No blood. Had I missed again? I took out my flashlight and looked over the area again. This time, I saw a splotch of blood in the wet leaves. Just then, I heard Mike yelling from the bottom of the ridge, "Get on down here and see this buck!" I ran down the hill to where Mike was standing and saw my trophy lying there in all his regal splendor.

I stayed with the deer while Mike went back to camp for the ATV. When we put the buck up on the back rack of our ATV, the carrying rack broke free from the frame. How were we going to get this deer back to camp over two miles of mostly uphill terrain? The rain had still not let up, either. I asked Mike if anyone was at camp. "No," he said, explaining that ours were the only pins on the board. A sickening feeling crept over me. What were we going to do?

Standing there in the driving rain, I noticed that I was starting to feel weak. It must be the rain and the anxiety, I thought to myself. It was late, close to 8:00 p.m., and one of us was going to have to walk out. How could this happen on what was supposed to be a joyous occasion?

Mike began strapping the buck to the seat of the ATV; we would walk it out. Really feeling weak and giddy, I didn't relish the thought of walking back to camp in this weather and in my condition. Then, as the wind howled through the trees, I thought I heard someone calling my name. Mike said that it was the wind. I heard it again and hollered back but didn't get an answer. Maybe it *had* been the wind, I thought to myself as my hopes faded. When I heard it again, I put all I had into my voice and bellowed back. This time I got an answer. I heard an ATV start up and saw a headlight piercing the darkness and coming down the road toward us. My heart leapt with joy!

Kevin had come looking for us. Approaching us, he saw the buck, gave me a congratulatory hug and began telling the story of how he had come to look for us. He had left his stand at dark, gone back to camp and had seen our truck there and our pins in the board. Wet and cold, he left for home but thought to himself, "Would those guys leave me down there by myself?" He turned around, came back to camp and unloaded his ATV. Though he really didn't know where we were since he had never been down in our area before, off he went into the cold rainy night, searching for us. Taking the first road on the left that he came to, he had hoped to find us somewhere along the road as he really didn't know where he was going. When he got to the end of the road, he shut the ATV motor off and started yelling, into the loud wind. He was really surprised to find us.

Putting the buck on Kevin's ATV, Mike and I doubled up on the seat of our ATV and finally made our way back to camp. When we got home, Jeanne, my wife, noticed that I was pale and white-looking and asked me if I was sick. Explaining that I wasn't feeling well, I started peeling off my layers of clothing. That's when I discovered the reason for the way I was feeling.

When I pulled off my rubber boot, it was filled with blood. Earlier, I had thought there was water in my boot, but since it was warm, I didn't give it any further thought. There was blood from my left knee down, but I had thought it was from cleaning the buck. I continued to take off three layers of blood-drenched clothing. When I pulled off my long johns and sock, I discovered I had somehow knocked a hole in my leg and perforated a varicose vein. The blood was shooting out in a steady stream. Jeanne put a compress on the wound and called a lady in our church who also was the director of nursing at the university. She told us to continue holding the compress to stop the bleeding. That did the trick. When she asked me how much blood I had lost, I replied, "a boot-full, four pantlegs full and a sock full plus about half a pint on the floor." She told me I was lucky and told me something to tell Kevin the next time I saw him.

Kevin called the next day to ask how things were going and to see if I was still sick. I told him what the nursing director told me. "Wally, you were bleeding to death and didn't know it. If your friend hadn't turned around and come looking for you, you probably would have bled to death trying to walk out of those woods. Thank that young man."

There was silence on the end of Kevin's line before he said, "You would have done the same for me."

A few days later, when it was safe for me to return to the woods, I went back down to our hunt camp and told the guys what Kevin had done for me. He wasn't there while I was telling the story. Around noon, he came wandering back to the camp, and it was a sight to behold. You see, Kevin is a little guy, about five foot four and 125 pounds with bright blue eyes and a thick, bushy beard. Me, well, I'm six feet tall and 360 pounds. When he got near me, I picked him up and gave him a big hug and called him "my blue-eyed, bushy-bearded guardian angel." We all had a laugh about that, and I always remember the day David saved Goliath.

That year, I won the club trophy for the biggest buck and Kevin got a special lifesaver award. At the awards banquet, Kevin asked me for a blessing so he could win the big buck trophy next year. I put my arm around him and told him, "God watches over those who help his own."

On the very last day of the following deer season season, Kevin ran up to me saying, "Your blessing worked!" I looked over his shoulder to see the guys admiring a huge ten-point buck that would eventually take that year's big buck trophy.

"Mr. Parise, There's the Deer"

by Marc Parise
Moline, Illinois

My first deer hunt took place in 1991. I was in the stand on one of the first days of the Illinois shotgun season with one of my buddy's ten-year-old twin daughters. Emily was as excited as I was to be hunting, even though I had the only gun. We were at the edge of a hedgerow between two cornfields. Emily was watching the north field, and I was watching to the south.

At 7:30 a.m., Emily tugged on my coat. "Mr. Parise, there's the deer."

Sure enough, a nice buck was cutting the corner of the cornfield from the hedgerow to the woods. I turned around slowly, put the sight on his shoulder, pulled the trigger, and the deer went down at 40 yards.

We both sat in the stand, amazed at what had just happened. Emily scurried down the ladder as I unloaded the gun and lowered it to the ground. By the time I got out of the stand, she was counting the points on the antlers.

"How many points?" I asked as I ran toward the buck.

"Seven on each side!" she answered.

I fell to my knees at the head of the animal and counted the points five times until I got fourteen two times in a row.

The deer field dressed at 205 pounds, and all the plaque on the shoulder mount says is, "Mr. Parise, there's the deer."

Big, Bad Boar

by Ken White
Abilene, Texas

I remember turning eight years old in south Florida. Gramps and I had been hunting buddies for years, or so it seemed. He had given me a .410 shotgun, and now I was ready to graduate from rabbits to big game.

My opportunity came by way of Gramps' friend, Old Pete, who owned a truck farm nearby. At the back of the property was a fair-sized lake with an island in the center. There lived the big, bad boar—the giant feral hog who would swim ashore at night, root up a substantial portion of the crop, then return to his island sanctuary. He was so big, and so mean, that all the hired hands were afraid of him. As a result, Old Pete asked Gramps and I to accompany him on a special hunt to kill "Boss Hog."

The morning of the hunt, we set out in Old Pete's airboat. It was a good vessel for hog hunting, as it would allow us to get close to shore. If we got into trouble, we could return to the water quickly. On the downside, the hull was made of lightweight aluminum, which a boar could easily gouge with his tusks.

Because the island was so close to the fields, a high-powered rifle would have endangered the farm workers. For this reason, Gramps had decided to hunt with this two nine-shot pistols. Having been a member of the Philadelphia Police Pistol Team, he was an expert marksman. Now he stood ready with his two .22 caliber H&Rs, one in each hand. Old Pete was not comfortable having a gun-toting eight-year-old along, so I had come unarmed to observe and help out as best I could.

As we approached the island, Old Pete cut the engine and we glided silently to shore. Only a few seconds elapsed before we heard the monster crashing through the palmettos. He came charging across the beach, heading directly toward us. Gramps hopped ashore and began firing both guns in rapid succession. From my position as a spotter, I could see numerous hits bouncing off the huge hog, but he was still 100 yards away and closing quickly. Gramps emptied all 18 chambers before taking refuge on the airboat to reload.

Old Pete was madly trying to restart the engine. By now, the boar had reached us and was ramming the boat. The lightweight vessel was tipping wildly as Gramps tried to reload the loose rounds from his pocket.

In his panic, Old Pete had flooded the engine, so he yelled to me to get his shotgun. As the boar continued his attack, I searched for the gun, with Old Pete screaming all the while. Finally, I spied it in a scabbard that was tied to the motor cage. It was a 20 gauge double barrel with two triggers, a type I was not familiar with.

I tried to hand the gun to Gramps, but he was still struggling to reload. With every ram of the boar's tusks, the boat tipped again. Old Pete was nearing hysteria.

"Shoot him! Shoot the S.O.B.!!!" he screamed.

I steadied the gun on the side of the boat and looked into two mean, mad hog eyes. I knew it was now or never. Aiming point blank at the boar's head, I pulled both triggers at once.

With one loud BOOM, a force I had never felt before threw me backward onto the deck. Dazed, I picked myself up and shook my head in disbelief. I had never fired such a gun before, but now I knew why it had two triggers. Nearby, I saw the result of the gun's power—the dead beast lying in the water.

After we had spent a few minutes hooting and hollering in glee at our victory, Old Pete started the obstinate airboat and we headed for home. The farmhands were sent to retrieve our prize, which became the main entree at a pork barbecue later that summer.

The First Deer

by Nathan Jacobs
Ponca City, Oklahoma

When I was about five years old, Dad started taking me with him on deer hunting trips. The Oklahoma whitetail gun season started the Saturday before Thanksgiving and ended the Sunday after. My parents would take me out of school the Thursday before the season started. Dad and I would pack the 15-foot travel trailer and head out into the woods. We would stay there until the end of the season.

We would camp and hunt on public land. In those days, I was not big enough to carry a deer rifle. However, I could already shoot, and Dad had taught me gun safety. I would sit on the stand as long as I could, then go back to camp.

I was about nine years old when I decided that I could handle Dad's .30-30. He took me out to an old rock quarry (we didn't have access to a range). Since we had not discovered treestands yet, Dad had me lie on the ground in a prone shooter's position. I will never forget that first shot. I slid backward in the gravel for a couple of feet. My shoulder hurt so bad that a tear came to my eye, but I did not want to disappoint my dad. I worked the lever and prepared to fire again when Dad said, "If once was enough, you don't have to shoot again. I won't think any less of you." That's when I really started to cry and gave him the gun back.

Dad bought another gun that year, one that I could handle, and I started hunting for real, but I didn't get a deer. A couple of years later, I started shooting that .30-30 on my own. I carried it as much as I did the other. I really wanted to shoot my first deer with that old .30-30, just like Dad did several years before me.

When I was a senior in high school, Dad and his friend, Lewis, found some private land to hunt on. This was near a town called Gray Horse, about an hour's drive from our hometown of Ponca City. I didn't get to hunt that year, but there was no stopping me the next year.

The stand I had for opening day was a tree in the middle of an open field. I chose the old .30-30, even though I knew the open sights were not the best choice for my hunting position. It was clear and cool that morning. We had decided to meet back at the truck at 9:00 a.m. By 8:00 a.m., it had started to drizzle, the wind was blowing and it was very cold. Also, I had to pee really bad. I stayed put as long as I could stand it. Just before 9:00 a.m., I got out of the tree. After I did my business, I put my gear together, then I saw Dad walking back to the truck (he was about 500 yards south of me).

I started away from my tree, but wanted to see how close to me a doe had been earlier. As I started pacing distance off to the north, a deer popped over a hill to my left. I stopped. There I was with open sights, no tree to use as a rest, and I stood right out in the open.

The deer bounced toward me. As he looked toward Dad, I saw the antlers. My mind was screaming, "A buck! What do I do now?"

I thumbed back the hammer and took aim. As I calmed, I decided that as long as he was coming to me I'd wait to shoot. I just held the sights on my target and waited for what seemed like an eternity. Suddenly, the deer locked his front legs and stopped. I squeezed the trigger. I watched the hammer fall. There was no loud, ear-splitting bang. There was no shoulder-bruising kick. The gun must have misfired!

My worst fear had been realized. But the deer had slipped in the mud. I still had a chance! I worked the lever and put another shell in. I knew where the deer was but could not see him. I waited, and waited, and waited. He wasn't getting up. What was going on? I finally got the nerve to look away from the deer and look at the ground. There was the empty casing I had ejected from my gun. The deer didn't get up because I had shot him!

I looked for Dad. There he stood, looking at me like I was an idiot. By then I was jumping up and down and trying to wave him over. He gathered his gear and started toward me. About halfway there, he was met by Lewis, who had come out of the woods at a dead run. Dad didn't know I had shot, Lewis thought I had shot myself by accident.

When they finally got to where I was, Dad asked me, "What did you want to show us?" All I could do was point and shout, "I shot a deer!"

Dad and Lewis checked the deer. Then Dad checked the distance. The deer was about 130 yards away from me when I shot him. He was a seven-point. The official weight was 100 pounds. I think Dad was more proud than I was.

I owe that hunt and many others to my dad, Dave Jacobs. He has those antlers hanging in his den with all his antlers. Thanks to Dad, I learned to hunt and shoot very well. He also taught me to really enjoy the outdoors and the wildlife that I find there. Every year I go hunting for the meat. After I get a deer, I return to the woods to spend the rest of my vacation. The deer I shoot then, I shoot with a 35mm camera.

Elk Camp with Dad

by Chuck Richardson
Belgrade, Montana

Back in the early part of 1984, Dad turned 68 years young. In a conversation one afternoon, he brought up elk hunting. He talked about northeastern Oregon around the town of John Day. Dad operated a bulldozer when he worked with a logging operation around Sumpter. He said he had seen several nice bull elk when he was working, and a few of the men he worked with had taken a bull elk during previous elk seasons.

Dad always talked about the beauty and the majestic grace of a big bull elk as it disappeared in the forest like a ghost.

I have two brothers. My youngest brother, Dan, was serving in the United States Marine Corps at the time. My middle brother is Ron, and I, Chuck, am the eldest.

Dad, Ron and I decided we would go elk hunting during Oregon's early season. So, we made plans and gathered our food and supplies. The weather in this area can turn very bad, so we planned for the worst.

By the time the Big Day came to set off on our journey of approximately 1,000 miles round trip, there was Dad and Mom, Ron and his wife, Ron's brother-in-law, Ron's son, my wife, my son and me. We were all avid hunters, but this was our first elk hunt.

The trip to our camp area went very well, and we were all very excited. With Dad's outdoors experience, we set up a very safe camp that was geared for any bad weather. Our camp was along the Burnt River and close to the main road that runs between John Day and Baker.

The nights around the camp stove were priceless—the stories and the laughter, the planning for the next day's hunt.

On one of our daily outings, we left camp before daylight. Dad was hauling five of us guys up on a high ridge line that had five or six long ridges running back to or close to camp. Dad dropped us off so that we could spread out and hunt back to camp. Dad would go back down the main Burnt River road and pick us up as we came down the hunt from the top to the pickup points, which was approximately six to eight miles. About two miles into the hunt, I heard Dad calling my name on the walkie talkie I had been carrying for safety. I heard him say, "Chuck, I have an elk down and I need help."

Ron's brother-in-law and I got to Dad as soon as we could. We helped him field dress the bull elk and get it loaded.

The nine of us came home with many happy memories, but my greatest memory was that 68-year-old young fellow, my dad, who had his dream come true when he harvested his first bull elk.

A Tribute to my Dad, Jack A. Cornell (1921-1985)

by Chris Cornell
St. Johns, Michigan

You taught me many things. Some I learned well, some I did not. The things I liked best —and the things I'll continue to remember for the rest of my life—were the things we did together. Hunting and fishing especially.

I remember those times at the cabin when you could have been with the guys, but you took me along and bought me coloring books. Then the next day, we would go to the woods. You with your rifle, me with my BB gun. I understand now why you didn't get any deer. I was making too much noise chasing and shooting at red squirrels with my BB gun.

It was a real disappointment when you, Uncle Clare, Uncle Russell and Raymond took off for the cabin on Thanksgiving weekend to deer-hunt. I would stay behind.

Finally the day came when I was able to hunt for deer just like you. I don't remember much about that day, only that I didn't sleep hardly a wink. That was 1965. In 1966, I got a doe. And a few days later I shot a buck. You weren't there, but when you got home you said, "I should kick your butt for not staying where I told you to, but I can't believe you got that buck."

We had a dry spell until 1975. I was in the Army for two and a half hunting seasons. I guess we'll call that buck our deer, seeing we both shot at it and I got it with your 16 gauge. We worked for it, gutted it and dragged it together. He was a dandy.

I still remember the time we headed to the cabin for a weekend hunt. We were unloading the food, guns, and hunting clothes; everything was there except your hunting clothes. They were still hanging in the closet at home. We made a quick trip home and got back to the cabin around 2:30 a.m. It was a short night's sleep, but we had a good laugh about it.

1983 was our year. November 15, we both had our deer by 10:30 a.m. They were baldies, but they looked good hanging in the tree together.

1984 was our last hunting season together. We were at the cabin for opening day with Uncle Art. It rained. When I came to pick you up, you were standing under that pine tree on the Bear Road, looking cold and wet. The rain turned to snow, and later that day I got a shot at a piebald back on the hill. Little did we know it, but it would be the last time we would be standing on the hill together, side by side, or that it would be our last opening day together.

Since then, your granddaughters have started hunting. One by one. I've taken them to the cabin for a day of hunting every year. I want them to experience the great northwoods and the things you passed on to me. The hill isn't quite the same. A forest fire got some of the top, and they clear-cut some of it, too. Some of the property has been sold, and the back road in has been closed off by the owners.

November 15, 1985—I headed for the woods and thorns this morning. There is an empty spot in the woods today. It is the first opening day without you in 20 years. It is the first time the 35 has been in the northwoods since you last carried it in 1984. Thirty-three years of trying, and I finally bring one home from the Roscommon. He didn't come from the hill, but he is a nice seven-point. He is hanging on the wall as a tribute to you, Dad. For the man and person you were.

It's just my way of saying thank you for your patience, understanding and teachings. Teaching me how to be a sportsman and that the most important thing is to enjoy God's creation and the comradeship of family and friends. For showing me your appreciation and heritage of the woods and the great sport of hunting. I know you are in the woods with me on every hunt. I feel your presence and can see your smile and hear your laugh. Thank you for being my dad and my best friend.

FIRST HUNTS TO REMEMBER

Hunting firsts create memories that last a lifetime ... and beyond, if the story has been told often enough and well enough.

What hunter can forget the heart-leap at finding his or her first buck in the autumn leaves? Or a mallard drake tumbling through the air after so many other misses? Or a pheasant rooster cackling wildly as he flushes into the setting sun and then falls in a puff of feathers?

The settings and the game may change, but sooner or later it all comes together, and another hunter is born right out there in the midst of some sunrise or sunset, and our hunting heritage gets another boost ...

Sixteen Feet

by Myron Anderson
Suttons Bay, Michigan

My friend Todd and I hunted all forenoon and into the early after-noon. We had been hunting along the Yuba River, on 40 acres owned by Todd's dad. There wasn't any snow this opening day, and it was, at times, dark in the swamp. This made it harder to spot deer, but we didn't care. We were just glad to be outside with rifles in hand, wait-ing to see what adventures we would have this year. The area we hunted had rolling terrain with corn and hay fields on the hilltops, with hard-woods on the slopes and cedar swamps in many of the valleys.

The part of the swamp we were hunting had a large blow-down area. At times, we would be 15 feet off the ground, working our way along the trunks of cedar trees toppled by some angry wind. We prided ourselves on our ability to "sneak soundlessly" through this tangle of limbs, upturned roots and standing water. We could get surprisingly close to our quarry before making a mistake, and hear—and sometimes see—the deer disappearing deeper into the swamp.

When this happened, we would act angry and disappointed on the outside, but being teenagers, we were having the time of our lives. We could spend six hours going little more than 100 yards in that mess, and love every minute of it.

We stepped out of the swamp around 3:00 and walked up the hill to eat some lunch. We were still talking about the deer that darted out from beneath the tree we had been walking on, when Todd's dad, Chuck, and my younger brother, Bruce, came by. They had been hunting some of the hardwoods earlier, but hadn't seen any deer. We all exchanged the day's stories and prepared to head to our late afternoon stands.

Bruce and Chuck both sat in a field overlooking the swamp. Chuck sat next to some young spruce trees, and Bruce on the other side of the field, some 150 yards away to the north. Todd and I headed into the hardwoods bordering the field to the south.

The woods stood on a hillside that settled down to the low ground of the swamp. Fingers of cedar trees jutted out here and there, making an uneven line between the swamp and hardwoods. A two-track wound its way along, keeping the hillside separated from the low ground. Fifteen yards on the other side of the cedars ran the river; at this point, it was three yards wide and one deep.

I sat at the base of a large maple tree, halfway up the slope, some 30 yards from the two-track, looking toward the swamp.

It wasn't long until I heard deer crossing the river. It's one of those "physical" sounds that deer make, letting you know that they are right here! My heart leapt into my throat. Every sense was alert! No matter how many times I sit there and hear that sound, I always react the same way.

Those cedar trees may as well have been a block wall painted green. They shielded the deer behind their leafy exteriors. Once the deer cross the river, you can sit there until dark waiting for them to emerge from the thick cover.

I sat very still for 20 minutes, senses starting to dull, when suddenly I saw movement on the two-track right in front of me. I had my scope set on four power and raised my rifle to scan the area. Working the .30-06 back and forth, I saw nothing. I lowered the gun only to see a doe headed in my direction. She seemed not to notice me and walked right past me up the hill, not 20 feet away. Blinking my eyes to make sure I was seeing what I thought I saw, I turned to my right and watched her pass by, making her way up the hill and out of sight.

When I turned forward again, I couldn't believe my eyes! Standing broadside right in front of me—he looked huge! He just stood there. Finally, I came back to my senses and started to raise my rifle. With the Browning to my shoulder, I looked through the scope and could see nothing but a brown blur. My scope was on too high a power for a target this close. He just stood there. Abandoning the Redfield, I tried sighting down the side of the barrel. And he just stood there. This all took place in seconds, but seemed to take forever. Moving the rifle and trying to point it at his shoulder, I looked one more time into the scope. Was I aiming at the right spot? Did I see movement through the scope? I was out of time. I pulled the trigger.

The buck took off running, not up the hill or down toward the swamp, but straight ahead. I watched him go until he was out of sight. I was always told to wait before following a shot deer, to give it time to lie down. I tried to remain calm. I started to pace off to where the deer had stood ... 14 ... 15 ... 16 feet! As I stood there, I started to realize how close he had been. No wonder he seemed so big standing there. Replaying the whole series of events in my head, I was having trouble believing them. But the blood trail told me I wasn't dreaming.

The deer was the first I ever harvested. He field dressed at 155 pounds and had a nine-point rack with short tines and an inside spread of 20 inches.

As each November rolls around, I think back on that day with great fondness and look forward to the hunt to come. But no matter how many deer I take the rest of my life, I'll always remember the feel and excitement of that day, when a whitetail buck showed up at 16 feet!

Deer Camp Memory

by Ronald Keller
Rosendale, Wisconsin

This story happened during the 1995 deer season. Our group is usually made up of 12 to 14 hunters every year. That opening day, Bob, one of the hunters from our group, was going to hunt alone several miles away from everyone. Bob was fairly new at this game. I guess you could call him a novice.

He didn't have a rifle of his own, so he was using a spare rifle from one of the other hunters, which turned out to be a .30-30 Winchester. Bob was dropped off at about 6:00 in the morning, and the plan was that he would be picked back up at the end of the day. The guy that loaned him the rifle thought that seven shells would be ample ammo for the day's hunt, so Bob headed for his stand.

On the way to his stand, he heard a deer snort (which scared the heck out of him), and he wanted to load his rifle, but had been told beforehand to wait until he was safely up in his stand. His stand was about one mile from the road and about 12 feet up in a tree.

Bob reached his stand and safely climbed into it. He then loaded his rifle and waited for that big buck. After about two hours, he started to doze off, and thought maybe he should climb back down before he fell

226

out of the stand. He then leaned against the ladder and sort of fell asleep, until something woke him and he started to look around. There, standing in front of him—maybe 50 yards away—was a ten-point buck looking right at him. Bob very slowly raised his rifle to shoot, and missed with the first shot. The buck just stood there and let him shoot again and again. After six shots, the buck decided to make a run for cover and Bob fired his last shell, missing again, as the buck disappeared. That was the last time Bob saw the buck. He looked all over, but found no blood, no hair, no sign of a hit.

Bob had to sit on his stand for the rest of the day with an empty rifle. You can bet he will never hear the end of that one.

First Turkey Surprise

by Otie Kirbinzky
Doniphan, Missouri

The first morning of the Missouri spring turkey season was upon me. I had been so nervous that I had not slept the night before. It was 3:00 a.m., and my brother, Tom, and I were on our way to the woods. This was our first turkey hunt ever. Neither of us had called to, or even seen a wild turkey before. We had studied pictures and had listened to other hunters talk about turkey hunting. Turkey hunting had only been open a few years in Missouri at this time (way back in 1973) and very few hunters knew much about turkeys. We still felt confident. Being young and enthusiastic would make up for our lack of experience, we hoped.

We arrived at our hunting location before 4:00 a.m. and had a long wait. We discussed our strategy. My brother would call using a pill bottle with a balloon stretched over a cut-out lid. It sounded great to me. I would shoot, since I could not call. Tom explained how he would start calling and what I should do. He said not to move, to stay hidden, make sure the bird has a beard, and shoot for the head and neck only. Okay, I was ready.

Just before daylight we heard a distant gobble. We immediately set out in the direction of the gobble. We walked and stopped to listen every 200 yards or so, and soon we were near where we thought the turkey was roosting. We hid and waited for the turkey to fly down, which he did almost as soon as we arrived. The trouble was, he flew down in the opposite direction from where we were set up. Now what?

We waited, and soon he gobbled. We could tell he was on the next ridge. Tom said to come on, and away we walked fast to the next ridge. We had climbed almost to the top of the ridge and stopped to listen. The turkey gobbled. Tom said to hide and he would call. The only place I could find to hide was behind a fallen log. I laid down on my stomach, facing the turkey, with my gun in front of me. Tom called and the turkey answered. He called again and the turkey double gobbled. Again Tom called, and I could hear the turkey walking in the leaves. Then I saw him coming straight toward me. I could see his beard swinging as he walked. I was afraid to move. He got within 25 yards and stepped behind a big tree. When he did, I raised my gun. As he stepped out from behind the tree, he gobbled and looked right at me. I aimed at his head and pulled the trigger on my 12 gauge Browning. I remember seeing stars and blackness. Tom was yelling, "Did you get him?" All I could do was try to clear my head. Blood was covering my hands and gun. What was wrong? By this time, Tom was next to me and he began laughing. He said, "You should see your face!" My nose and mouth were cut and bleeding from the gun kicking me in the face. I had used a magnum load, and it had done its job at both ends. The turkey was dead and I was hurting. Tom laughed and said that we needed to get in and check the turkey, and get me to a doctor. I said no way. I would never live that down. After washing, I realized that I was not seriously hurt. Mostly my pride was injured. We both were so excited that we had our first turkey that only later did I remember to tell everyone not to lay on their stomachs when shooting at something, especially with a magnum load. All my other hunting buddies said they already knew that. I wished someone had told me. Instead, I got a first turkey surprise.

Bullwinkle

by Jesus Silva
Clear Lake, Wisconsin

I'll always remember the year Teresa, my wife, let "Bullwinkle" get away. Teresa never expressed any interest in hunting, so you can imagine my surprise when, a few days before deer season opened, she said she wanted to go hunting. Needless to say, she didn't get in much target practice.

Bullwinkle is the nicest, biggest hunk of buck I've ever seen that wasn't already hanging on someone else's wall. I've glimpsed him only a few times over the past six years. A few people know there's a big one around, but only one other neighbor has ever seen him. He saw him just standing out in an open field in the afternoon, the day after hunting season closed last year. Bullwinkle was probably laughing.

Well, my wife loved hunting. We mostly used treestands. We would get out before daybreak and sit until noonish, go home for a short break, then head out again. On the third day, on her way back, she noticed what she called giant tracks heading into a very small section of standing corn, and she insisted that we go back and she'd try and push something out for me. Now this was a tiny piece of corn, not near any woods, and I didn't want to bother, but she persisted, claiming again how big the tracks were. So back we went. I told her to wait on one end, and I'd go through the corn to get it over with.

I did see deer in there. A doe and fawn were laying down. What I didn't see was laying just in front of them—you guessed it. So there stood Teresa, and out tore Bullwinkle, right in front of her! Then he

turned, giving her a perfect broadside shot. If her gun would have been just a little longer, she could have poked him in the belly. She shot three times, but I don't know what at.

You can imagine how mad I was when I realized it was the real Bullwinkle. There was so much distance between his leaps, it was like he just disappeared. A hunter's wildest hunting fantasy couldn't have been any better than that opportunity, and she blew it.

I didn't get much sleep the next couple of nights, and she kept muttering, "I'm so mad, my blood's still boiling!"

She had hunting fever all winter, got her gun out in May and started practicing. She ended up being a pretty good shot. Bullwinkle must know that, because he hasn't jumped out in front of her since.

My Favorite Hunting Story

by Stuart Ashley
Traverse City, Michigan

Two friends and I had decided to leave school and go hunting for the weekend northwest of Tulsa, Oklahoma. Brian knew the area we were hunting well. I did not have an Oklahoma hunting license, and Tim had never been hunting and was eager to go for his first time, since he had just finished his Hunter's Education course.

Brian led Tim and I through the crisp, dark December morning to a tall creek bank overlooking an old field with a treeline around it. When Tim and I had settled in our hunting spot, the sunlight had started breaking through the trees enough to see potential areas where the deer would travel. I explained to Tim that the deer would come from our left down by a draw, or come from our right out of the treeline beside the creek bottom. Tim had worn a pair of coveralls and a stocking cap like Chuck Adams wears. I had worn a pair of jeans, shirt, and a jacket Brian had lent me. Neither one of us was really dressed for that morning excursion, but we were content and happy to be hunting.

At 7:15 a.m., a five-pointer came from our left, down by the draw, just the way I had explained to Tim. The five-point walked down into the creek and into some brush in the center and stopped just inside the brush. Tim was looking for the deer desperately through the Simmons scope mounted on the .30-06 Brian had lent him. The deer walked out of sight. I explained to Tim that when the deer was in the brush, he should be looking through the scope where the deer would walk out of the brush into sight and place the crosshair on the deer, then squeeze

232

the trigger. While I was explaining this to Tim, the deer walked back out to where he had crossed the creek, about 80 yards away. Tim raised the .30-06 back to his shoulder, looking for the deer through the scope. I was thinking, "Shoot the damn deer." Tim fired the rifle and shot just below him. The deer, in its confusion, turned and ran toward Tim and I, and quartered just to the left 40 yards away. "Tim, you missed the deer, shoot at it again." Tim fired the rifle a second time, hitting the deer a little far back. The deer ran busting through the brush, and climbed up the creek bank 60 yards away. At this point, I was so excited, I wanted to take the gun and shoot the deer myself, but I told him, "You hit the deer once. Shoot again." Tim leveled the .30-06 and fired a third time, hitting the deer in the front-left shoulder, dropping the deer where he stood. Tim and I were so excited, we almost did a crappie flop off the creek bank into the creek. When we finally settled down, Tim leaned over and whispered, "We need to wait at least 30 to 45 minutes before we go over to the deer." It was just what he had learned in his Hunter's Safety course. I told Tim, "No, I think that deer is dead."

Tim, congratulations on your first deer. It was a great experience for both of us, and thank you for my favorite hunting story.

Two Sons and a Father

by Richard Ambrose III
Akron, Ohio

I have been a hunter for eighteen years. I have many good stories, and plenty of sad ones, too, but I think and hope that this hunt will never be forgotten.

My two sons, Josh and Joe, had gone with me to deer hunt, and had hunted small game themselves. I did not rush them to hunt deer because I wanted them to learn all they could first.

This year was their first deer hunt. Josh was sixteen and Joe was fifteen. We left home on Sunday afternoon for our hunting camper. I told my wife that I would be happy if the boys got a chance to harvest their first deer.

We arose Monday for our hunt. Joe and I went one way, and Josh went another. Joe and I hunted about 75 yards from each other. We parted in the dark at 6:30 a.m. to beat the other hunters in the woods. About ten minutes later, a man walked right under my tree. I was in a treestand, so I flashed my flashlight at him and he left. I was hoping the boys would do well.

About 8:15, I saw the biggest deer of my life—a 14-point buck—so I shot it at about 20 yards. I was so excited, I could not express my joy. I tried to drag it out by myself, but it was too big. I yelled for Joe to come, because there was no way I was going to leave my buck. When Joe came down the hill, I stood in front of my buck to hide it, and when he reached me, I stepped aside. Joe got a grin on his face that stretched from ear to ear, and his eyes were wide open.

It took us a while to drag the deer out of the woods. There was a lot of shooting by now, so I told Joe to hurry back to his treestand. I hadn't seen Josh for a few hours, so I wanted to touch base with him. When I met up with him, I sat on the ground next to his tree, and while we were talking, I saw a deer coming up the hill, right at us. I told Josh to get ready, and at 15 yards, Josh harvested his first deer. After helping Josh get his button buck back to camp, I grabbed a sandwich and went to find Joe. As I was walking up the road, Joe was coming toward me with a big grin on his face. He said he had gotten his first deer, which was a button buck, and all the work was done. I was tired by now, so Josh and Joe had to drag this one out together. We were done hunting by noon on the first day of the season. Not bad for a first hunt, and good memories. I think the boys are hooked on hunting now.

Thanks, Uncle

by Charles Way
Front Royal, Virginia

To say it had been a bad year in my life would be an understatement. Having to deal with my grandfather's death was the single most traumatic event of my life at the time, and remains so today, 14 years later. My grandfather, affectionately known as Pap, was truly an upstanding man. He devoted his life to educating young people, but probably more important, he devoted his life to being as good a husband, father and grandfather as anyone could hope to be. He was the type of man that possessed a wisdom about people and the world that is rare among others that I have come in contact with.

Shortly after his funeral, my grandfather's brother John, Uncle John to me, asked if I might like to go turkey hunting with him in the upcoming fall season. He didn't have to ask twice. I had never been turkey hunting before. My dad had taken me on several outings for squirrels and rabbits with little luck to speak of; his motivation for our hunting trips was solely to spend some quality time with his son doing something his son wanted to do. Hunting, fishing, shooting, tennis, mountain biking—I don't think the activity mattered much to Dad, only the time spent with his boys.

By the time the season was scheduled to open in late October, plans had already been made over the phone to have my parents drop me off at Uncle John's place and he would take it from there.

On our hour-long ride to my Uncle's hot spot, he gave me as complete a beginner's lesson in turkey hunting as I could have asked for. The topics of his talk ranged from the necessity to remain still, shot placement, calling techniques and safety procedures. This being a Saturday as well as the first day of the season, Uncle John insisted we wear blaze orange while moving.

Upon arriving at our destination, Uncle John pulled a Remington 1100 20-gauge from his trusty Jeepster. This would be the gun I was to use on this day. Before heading off on our pursuit, Uncle John taught me the proper workings of his semi-automatic 20 gauge. He made sure I knew the proper way to load and unload the gun, as well as the location and function of the safety.

As we started down the slightly worn trail away from the road, Uncle John handed me a half-full box of three-inch 20 gauge shells. "Sixes," he said. "Always load sixes." As we made our way further down the scantily used trail, the afternoon sun began to grow warm and I hoped we might flush a few grouse and Uncle John would let me have a try at one. Throughout the morning, I was assured of the presence of a large flock of turkeys in the area.

When we made our way to what would have been our first calling setup, we began to round a bend in the trail. As we did, I could not believe what I was about to see—turkeys everywhere along the trail. One after another filed out of the woodland onto the trail before us. I will not venture a guess at how many (the fondness of this memory has probably added to the number anyway).

Uncle John quickly nudged me into the thick brush that lined the small woodland trail. "Okay, Charlie, we'll hunker down and sneak up to the bend again to get a little closer," he whispered in my ear. We began to inch closer under the protection of the brush that lined the trail. After creeping what felt like 10 yards with the flock out of sight, Uncle John pulled me back onto the trail and whispered a new command in my right ear. "Cut loose, Charlie!" The bead of the 20 gauge came up and stopped at the base of the neck of the first turkey I saw—safety off—and I pulled the trigger. Meanwhile my uncle, being a little more selective, singled out a slender young jake and in less time than it takes to read about it, I had harvested my first turkey. More importantly than the taking of game, a memory had been made and a lifelong passion had begun.

After my uncle and I placed our tags on our birds, I can't remember hitting the ground on the walk back to the Jeepster. I'll always remember the look on my grandmother's face when Uncle John and I hoisted those birds from his vehicle.

Other lessons taught to me by my uncle after the hunt included field dressing and wet plucking. Both tasks had been foreign to me until that point. Before my uncle left that day, I was given that Remington 1100 20 gauge used on that first turkey hunt. I really felt, at that point, that just saying thank you was not enough, but it was all that a 15-year-old kid had to give in return for this gift of experience.

The events of my first turkey hunt happened some 14 years ago, but I can remember the details of that warm day in late October as if it were last weekend. I have eagerly awaited every turkey season, spring and fall, since that day. I can't find the words to state how I enjoy spending time in the outdoors scouting, hunting and enjoying wild turkeys.

I think back to my first turkey hunt and the many that have followed with appreciation for the gift of the outdoors. I have come to recognize wildlife, wild places and the time spent enjoying them, as gifts. As with all gifts, they must be given, and who to thank for the experience of these natural gifts? Fathers, uncles, brothers, mothers, friends, Almighty God—the list is endless. Maybe I'll get started. Thanks, Uncle.

My First Deer

by Chris Nelson
Hartland, Wisconsin

I had graduated from a Hunter's Safety program in March of that year. It was my first year going deer hunting with a firearm. I was very excited. My dad said that we would have a lot of fun.

We woke up on Friday the 21st of November and got packed. At about 10:00 a.m., we started up to the cabin. The cabin was near Black River Falls, Wisconsin. My uncle Steve owned the cabin and 120 acres of land.

When we got there, my uncle Mike, my cousin Matt and our friends Lee and Tim were there. My uncle and cousin had been up there since early Thursday. About four hours later the other five members of our hunting party arrived at the cabin.

At 10:00 p.m., the elders of the party went to bed, but not me! I stayed up until about 12:00 talking and thinking about a big buck that I would love to shoot.

In the morning at 5:00 we got up. Less than an hour later, everybody was prepared to go to their stands. It took about half an hour to get to my dad's stand. At 6:30, I was in position. The first thing I did was load the rifle I was using. It was a .44 caliber Ruger carbine semi-automatic with a scope that I borrowed from my uncle Jim. I stood on the ground by a tree about fifty yards from my dad.

It was too dark to shoot, so we had to wait a while. I quietly stood around for an hour, then I heard some noise, but I didn't see anything. I was standing on the ground for another hour and turned around and saw a good-sized deer. I thought it was a doe, but I decided to shoot at it anyway because I was able to take either a buck or a doe. I put the rifle to my shoulder, put the crosshairs on the shoulder of the deer and pulled the trigger once. Boom! The deer ran.

I started walking to get the deer, but my dad got down from his stand and told me to wait. Ten minutes later, we tried to find blood or fur. Dad asked me where the deer was when I shot, and I wasn't sure. I was nervous because of all the excitement. Later, we started walking southeast, in the direction my dad had seen the deer run. He had heard a loud crashing sound moments after the deer left my sight. After about 85 yards we found the deer. We found out that it was a spike buck. Then we tagged and gutted the buck.

We took my buck back to the cabin and I told everybody about my first deer. Then I got to tease my dad until Sunday when he shot his buck.

A Morning of Memories

by Tom Head
Pollock, Missouri

I glanced down at my watch. It was 6:09 a.m., far too early for a young boy and his father to be sitting under a tree on a cold Saturday morning in November. Yet that was where we were, and both of us were glad to be there. Because not only was this the first morning of Missouri deer season, but it was also the first day of my deer hunting career.

In the chill of the predawn darkness, my mind wandered back in time to when I was four years old. That year I had begged my father to take me with him when he went hunting. One evening during deer season he finally gave in, and since we were going hunting, I had to take along my deer gun—a plastic toy army rifle. Upon mounting our trusty steed, a 1981 Honda 110 three-wheeler, we headed down to watch the edge along one of our corn fields. When we rounded a corner, Dad immediately spotted our quarry. Minutes later, after he had explained to me exactly where to look for the now restless creatures, I finally found them in the sights of my weapon. In the meantime, Dad had uncased, loaded, and was then preparing to shoot one of the deer that was running across the field and away from us. After being told to be quiet for the eleventh time in the last five minutes, I watched as the animals made their way into the timber surrounding the crop ground. At the crack of the rifle shot, I hollered, "Shoot again, Dad! Ya missed! Shoot again!" Since I couldn't see the deer that had fallen, I was sure that he had missed. However, he assured me that he had not. The argument that ensued between the two of us finally ended when we remounted

241

and drove across the field to where the deer lay. I said it was my shot that hit the deer, but he still won't admit that it was.

As I sat shivering, my mind snapped back to November 1991, and I said to myself, "This is nothing like what I had expected. We're deer hunting. There should be deer jumping out of the timber all around us to shoot at like on the TV shows. Where are they? Man, it's cold! I could be at home in bed, asleep. What are we doing out here?" Then Dad's elbow contacts my side, followed by, "Sit still," in a tone that would make a fence post jump. I sat still for the next 20 minutes, give or take 15. At about 7:30, my feet were beginning to feel like blocks of ice, and I wanted to go back to the house. When we turned around, I saw a deer standing not more than 100 yards behind us. Quietly, we moved around so that my .243 was pointed at the deer as my guide (Dad) whispered a few final instructions. I prepared myself for the shot, then BANG. I would like to say that this lone shot ended my hunt. However, that was not the case. It took one more shot before I was able to tag my first deer.

On the second day we sat under the same tree as we had the day before. As the sun cleared the hill behind us, its rays began to illuminate a weedy area and the bean field that it surrounded. At 7:00 a.m., we could see something moving in the light of the rising sun, almost half a mile west of us in the weeds. It only took one look through the binoculars to identify it as a buck deer. The next 30 minutes seemed to take the place of hours as the animal made its way toward us. Just before the beast entered the effective range of my rifle, he disappeared into the brush along the field. For a moment, one 11-year-old boy was almost in tears, until the buck stepped out on our side of a thicket that stuck out into the field. The moment my prey came in sight the second time, my heart began to race, my nerves and muscles became tense and my palms began to sweat. Just to make sure that I would not make a mistake, my guide reminded me of everything that I needed to do, assured me that I would do well, and tried to keep me calm. The next two minutes seemed to take all morning as the magnificent animal made his way toward our concealed location under a small pin oak tree. Through the scope on my rifle, I could see each hair on his body as he paused to nibble at some spilled soybeans. A gentle nudge on my shoulder meant that the time was right and that I should shoot. For a moment, time stood still as a single shot shattered the silence on a crisp Sunday morning. The bullet entered through the deer's chest, causing him to spin and run toward a fencerow. Before he could jump over the obstruction, he fell, tangling his antlers in the weeds, wire and brush.

After the shot we gathered our equipment and started toward the spot where he disappeared into the weeds. Wading through the thick undergrowth, we quickly found the buck lying on his side. By 8:30, we had field dressed the small eight-point, walked back to the truck, then drove back home to get the tractor and carry-all to return for the deer.

Looking back on that day, I'm not sure who was more proud, my father or me. Both of us took a huge step forward that day; I was one step closer to becoming an adult, and he changed from being the booming voice who constantly had to remind me to feed the dogs, to a faithful hunting companion and best friend. Since then, we have shared many other hunting trips, and made many memories, but this will always be my favorite.

Hunting with Dad

by Michael Windbeck
Lehighton, Pennsylvania

My first year hunting deer in Pennsylvania was my best. My dad and I built a hunting stand together in the summer, preparing for the big day. This stand was more like a small house. We could sit inside if it rained, or sit on the roof and get a bird's eye view of the 15-acre cornfield. All around this field was woodland. I dreamed of the first day for months. Finally the big day arrived. My dad and I walked to the stand, and I could feel the jitters. When we got to the stand, I climbed up on top, but my dad decided to sit inside. As it started to get light, my heart started to pound harder with every noise I heard. Around 7:30 a.m., a deer walked out of the corner of the woods and into the cornfield. I could see the antlers on his head. My heart was racing so fast that I thought the deer could hear it. Finally, I put the scope on him at 75 yards and shot. He dropped to the ground instantly. My dad jumped out of the stand and yelled, "Did it have antlers?" I said yes, but he asked again. He watched the deer until I got down from the stand, and we walked out to take a look at it. As we walked out, all I could think of was, "Do not get up, deer." My dad kept asking me, "Did it have antlers?"

When we got there, the first thing my dad did was look at the head to make sure it had antlers. Then, he walked over and shook my hand to congratulate me on my first eight-point buck. I was so excited, I did not know what to do next. After my dad helped me fill out the tag, he told me to get out the knife and gut it. I had gutted rabbits and squirrels before, but this was my first deer. As I poked the knife into the deer, I did the wrong thing. I pushed hard, and pushed the knife into the stomach, which made me turn green! But I kept on going until I had the deer gutted.

I have gotten many deer since that day, but I will always remember my dad and I hunting together that day. I can only hope that I can share a day like this with my son when he is old enough. My dad and I spent many hours hunting, sometimes getting nothing, but I would never trade in one of those days for anything.

My First Deer Hunt

by Gail Kniska
Hurley, Wisconsin

I was 14 years old and somewhat of a tomboy. I idolized my dad, and while listening to him and some of my uncles and cousins discussing the upcoming deer season, I decided I wanted to try deer hunting. I approached my dad with my request to take me on a hunt. I remember he beamed, and I knew instantly he was very happy with my request. I had no brothers and my dad had always instructed me on woods lore, deer tracks and all other sorts of outdoor know-how. My dad and I often spent time in the field target shooting, and I had been carefully instructed on safety.

There were two big problems. I had no hunting apparel, and no gun. My dad set out to attempt to borrow the necessary equipment. The day before the season began, we went out to collect my borrowed gear: a black and red, heavy wool coat, a red wool cap with ear flaps, green wool hunting pants, and a pair of Sorel boots, two sizes too big. Laughing all the while, my dad and I agreed I certainly looked like one of the "boys." Finally, we visited a neighbor to collect my gun. Little did I know, but my dad had arranged for them to give me a heavy old flintlock rifle, which was about 4 feet long and felt like it weighed a ton. I knew I could never carry it around all day, let alone aim it to shoot anything, but I attempted a smile and took the gun, murmuring a thank you. As my dad could probably tell, I was about to burst into tears. He suddenly produced a nice, light .30-30 rifle, and suggested I

might like that better. Instantly, I realized the joke was on me, and gladly accepted the gun from my smiling father.

Opening morning dawned cold and crisp. My dad and I donned our hunting gear, packed sandwiches and coffee, and set out on our hunt. We walked around a section of woodland slowly (mostly, I think, because I could scarcely move with all the heavy clothes), but not finding any sign of deer movement. We decided to follow some nearby railroad tracks. Walking along, we came upon a friend of my dad's, who proceeded to tell us (in some very colorful language) of the deer he had just missed. Suddenly the man began to unzip his trousers to relieve himself, and my dad almost choked because he realized that the man had no idea I was a girl! Dad quickly stopped him, and I had to choke

247

back my laughter as he suddenly turned a brilliant shade of red. Apologizing, he quickly went off into the woods. My dad and I laughed, and although we both later got a case of buck fever and never did get our deer, we thoroughly enjoyed our hunt.

I didn't hunt again for about 20 years, but in the last ten years I have taken up the sport again. Each time I dress for the woods, I think of that first hunt and thank my dad for giving me the opportunity to learn about hunting in days when girls just didn't do that.

My First Deer

by Russ Luchenbill
Owasso, Minnesota

When the alarm finally sounded at 4:30 a.m. after a very sleepless night, I jumped out of bed with the excitement of the day's coming hunt. Trying not to wake my wife, I scurried around in the dark for the clothes that I set out the night before. With this accomplished, I began to pack my backpack with nothing more than the bare essentials: coffee, doughnuts, milk, radio, knife, magazine, an extra coat and my binoculars. When I headed out the door at 5:00, I almost forgot to take my gun. Convinced that I had everything I needed, I drove the eight miles to the location where I intended to hunt for the day. Along the way, I hoped for success because I had never hunted this property before.

I arrived at my destination and began the long journey back to my blind, one that I had built previously along a very narrow, slow-flowing river. My time in the blind passed quickly. I looked at my watch. It was almost 8:00, and time for the morning news and some milk and doughnuts for a snack.

I never dreamed that the milk would send chills through my already cold body. With the news over, I put the radio away, not wanting to listen to any music. Then I had my last cup of coffee to warm myself back up. With all that I had drunk, I decided to stand and relieve the pressure building in my bladder. While doing this, I glanced behind me. Straight across the river, not 20 yards away was my dream—a nice buck with his head down, following a trail along the riverbank. I took careful aim with my new Remington 1100 20 gauge and fired. The buck rolled completely over and ran off into the swamp.

Now faced with the deer on one side of the river and me on the other, I started looking for a place to cross over. I started going upstream until I found a small tree lying most of the way across the river. After unloading my gun and balancing carefully, I began to cross on the tree limb until it ended. I knew I had to jump, but before I could the limb snapped in two and I fell into the river with my gun in hand. Climbing out on the other side, with the air temperature about 20 degrees, I knew now what real cold was.

Still excited about the deer, I began tracking. Following a faint blood trail is not easy, but I came upon a small ditch that I slid down into. Imagine my surprise when I found water in the bottom. I climbed out the other side and tripped on a branch, which caused me to fall and scrape my face on a barbed wire fence. Losing some of my enthusiasm, I continued tracking until I lost the trail in the swamp. Knowing better than to give up, I kept looking. Trying to find any small sign to follow, I reached the far side of the swamp. I was glad to find a large grassy area that allowed me to see for a distance.

Not having any idea where to start, I began a back-and-forth pattern, searching for signs of the deer. More than three-quarters of the way through, I was getting tired and cold. Looking for a place to rest, I spotted an old fallen tree just a little ways off in the corner of the grass field. I started to head that way to take a rest, but the closer I got, I saw that a deer was lying next to the tree. With my gun still frozen from the fall in the river, I was not in a promising position. Continuing to watch the deer, I realized that it was not moving. I started to approach slowly and with caution. I was full of excitement, knowing that I had found the deer I was looking for. As I finally reached the tree, the deer still was not moving. After 14 years of hunting, I was now standing over my first deer harvest, but was left wondering how I was going to get it back to the car.

After tagging the deer, I started to drag the buck out of the grass field while thinking about the river that I had to cross. But before I could reach the river, I would have to get through the swamp first. I made it to the riverbank and decided that I would leave the deer in the weeds and try to find someone to help me. Going upstream about a half a mile, I found a place to cross the river. I made the long hike back to the car after stopping at my blind to pick up my camp stool and day pack. As I was walking back, I continued to reminisce about the morning's hunt.

After changing my wet, frozen clothes, I drove over to get my brother Mike for his help dragging my deer out of the woods. When Mike and I reached the river, I told him to wait while I went upstream, crossed the river, then came back downstream to where the deer was. I tied the rope to the buck's antlers and threw the other end across the river to my brother so he could pull. Not wanting to make the hike upstream again to cross over, I decided to step on a branch that was partially over the river, then onto the deer and then to another branch to cross over. However, things did not go as smoothly as I planned. I made it to the deer but as I stepped on it, it rolled and I went back in the water. As I climbed out, my brother had already pulled the deer across the river and was laughing hysterically at me. When he was done laughing, he asked me why I had not dressed out the deer. I answered that I had been too excited. I field dressed the deer, and to my surprise, it made a big difference in dragging it. We continued to drag the deer to the truck, even though my pants were frozen stiff, making it hard to walk.

We arrived home and hung my five-point buck in the garage. After finishing the task, my brother turned to me and asked if it had been worth all the trouble. I told him yes, that it was a trophy in my eyes.

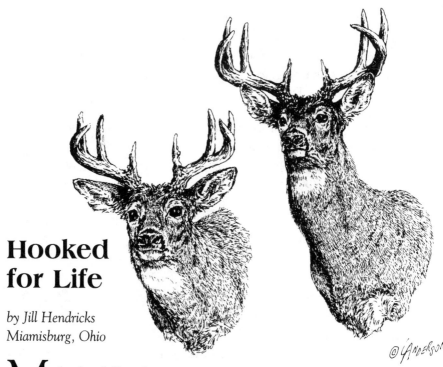

@ ANDERSON

Hooked for Life

by Jill Hendricks
Miamisburg, Ohio

My husband, Darrel, has gone deer hunting every year since we've been married. That's 16½ years. Each year, a week or two before his trip, hunting was all he would talk about. He would talk and plan and then talk and plan some more. I never understood how a person could be so excited about a deer hunting trip.

Last year, he mentioned that I should get my hunting license and go with him. We do a lot of fishing together, so I thought, "What the heck?" Having never had a hunting license before, I had to attend and pass a Hunter's Safety course. I spent an entire Saturday and Sunday in Lebanon, Ohio, at the safety program. Boy, did I study the handbook they gave us. All my hard work paid off in the end, though. I aced the test with a perfect score. Imagine my surprise when I returned home on Sunday evening with my Hunter's Safety Card, and my husband had a Remington 870 Express waiting for me. It was a 20 gauge pump with a 26-inch barrel.

Now there were two of us planning the hunting trip. We would talk and make a few plans each month. I think we started in August planning our trip. Finally, the big day came.

Opening day in Ohio was December 1. We hunted in Morgan County near Athens, Ohio. I was really surprised at how much more hilly southern Ohio is. The terrain seemed pretty rugged to me. I sure didn't want Darrel to be sorry that he brought me. I can honestly say I can hump those hills with the best of them.

We entered the woods before daybreak. Dressed in my hunter's orange, flashlight in hand and armed with my 870, I made my way to the spot I had cleared the day before. My husband made sure I was settled in and then with his 1187 ("the cannon") made his way to a nearby ridge. About 11:00 a.m., I heard Darrel fire his gun. I left my spot and went to see if he had been successful. When I got to him, he was so excited. He had shot an eight-point buck on the run. I was so excited for him. It was his first buck. If we had left right then, the trip would have been worth it.

At 3:00 that afternoon, back at my spot, I heard something creeping through the woods. When it came into the clearing and I saw it was a buck, I couldn't believe it. I didn't panic like I thought I might. Instead I just became real calm and determined. I waited until the buck was just about to the top of the ridge. The next leap he took would put him out of sight. I figured it was now or never. I raised my gun, aimed at the spot behind his shoulder and fired. Much to my excitement, he fell immediately. I had hit him exactly where I had aimed. When Darrel got to me and my deer, he was so excited for me.

My husband was so proud of my accomplishment, he put my picture in the *Miamisburg News*, our local paper. Now he says on next year's trip, if I'm successful again, I'll have to gut my own deer. As you can tell, I'm hooked!

First Squirrel

by Matt Allen
Athens, Pennsylvania

When my brother Tim turned 12 back in June 1977, he was all excited about going squirrel hunting for the first time. He and Dad headed out in the Blazer up the mountainside. They sat and waited for a squirrel. Suddenly there was a movement in a tree. Then another. Two squirrels were above them. Dad told Tim to pick one and take his time. Carefully, Tim took aim, fired, and down went one squirrel.

"Way to go, Tim," Dad said. "You just got your first squirrel. Now go get it."

As Tim went to pick up the squirrel, he saw the other one. Bursting with confidence, Tim quickly handed the squirrel to Dad and asked him if he would clean it while he went after the other one. Dad, being very proud of his firstborn son said, "Of course."

While Tim was sneaking up on the other squirrel, he heard Dad cry out in pain, "Son of a ...!" Tim, concerned about Dad and his heart condition, ran back to him and said, "Dad, are you OK? Is it your heart?"

Dad answered, "No, you darb, you handed me a live squirrel!"

My First Hunt

by Dan Nimtz
Niles, Michigan

It was a cold November morning when I set out to my blind. A lot of things were rushing through my head. Did I have everything for the day's hunt—flashlight, day pack, ammunition? But the most important question was, since this was my first year in the woods, would I see anything?

After a few hours in the blind, my fingers were already numb and my thermos of hot chocolate was empty. I was beginning to fall asleep when three does jumped out over a hill about 20 yards from me. I quickly awakened from my sleepiness and grabbed my Winchester .30-06 rifle. I fumbled with the rifle to get it out the blind window, and when I finally did, the deer were 200 yards down the field; but the noise I had made from fumbling with my gun must have made them stop, because when I shouldered the rifle, the largest doe of the bunch was standing broadside. I took close aim at the shoulder, although I was shaking very badly, and pulled the trigger.

I took a few deep breaths and quickly exited the blind. I hurriedly walked down the hill to inspect the area. When I approached the area where the deer had been, my heart sank as I unloaded my gun. There was no sign of a hit—no blood, no fur. My uncle said that I had cleanly missed the deer.

The next day I started fresh. I got plenty of sleep, and had a good breakfast. I made sure to bring extra supplies for the day's hunt, including a warmer pair of gloves. Also, this time I was using a friend's blind, but it was still on the same land. As time passed by, I couldn't help dozing off. Around 10:30, when I was half asleep, out ran 15 does! I again made a lot of noise getting my rifle out the window, but the situation was good. As I viewed the large field in front of me, I noticed that three does had stopped in the field in my line of sight. I looked through my scope and picked out what seemed to be a large doe at the edge of the field, about 175 yards away. I took aim at the shoulder, again shaking very badly, and took the shot. I missed! But the deer was still there, looking right at me. I quickly loaded another shell and took aim again. I slowly squeezed the trigger and the gun went off, throwing the gun's scope into my eye. I gave a shout of pain as I put the gun down. I realized that I hadn't had the gun tight to my shoulder, and that's why the scope had hit my eye. I sat back down in my chair, thinking I had missed that deer, too.

But I thought it was worth a look, so I exited the blind with my gun in hand, and started the trek to where the deer had been. I looked around intensely for five minutes, but I found no sign of a hit. Suddenly something white caught my eye as I turned around. I walked closer, and a deer started flopping up and down in the switch grass. I shouldered the rifle and walked closer, and sure enough, I had hit the deer. As I stepped into the clearing where it was laying, it died. I quickly poked the deer to make sure it really was dead, just like the hunting books I had read instructed. I ran over to my cousin's blind to inform him that I had downed a deer. An hour-and-a-half later, I was gutting my deer with my uncle. I had shot the deer in the stomach and the liver, which had caused the deer to trop in its tracks as it bled to death. We both realized that the deer was a button buck, and I was a little disappointed because I thought I was shooting at a nice doe. But my uncle said it was a nice sized button buck anyway, and I had to agree. Looking through a nine power scope with a 32mm objective at 175 yards makes it kind of hard to tell how big a deer really is, especially when you're excited and you know that this deer could be your first. Also, the buttons were covered by fur. I was proud of that deer, no matter the size, because it was my first deer in my first year of hunting.